The
INSTANT POT ELECTRIC

PRESSURE COOKER

COOKBOOK UK 200

Easy, quick and delicious recipes

Charlotte Morton

© 2023 C. Morton

Charlotte Morton

© 2022 C. Morton

Table of contents

Introduction

The pressure cooker is a kitchen utensil that is often used for cooking several foods. If you do not know this product yet, we will give you a short presentation.

Definition of pressure cooker and use

Better known as a pressure cooker, the pressure cooker is a metal container that closes hermetically using a lid with a steam release valve. It also has different kinds of names depending on each country, namely: the pressure cooker in Belgium, the Duromatic in Switzerland and the Presto in Quebec.

In particular, the pressure cooker is used to cook food under high pressure and thus reduce the cooking time. For example, if it takes 1.5 hours to tenderize the meat, it only takes 30 minutes for the pressure cooker to do the job.

Principle of the pressure cooker

As we said above, the pressure cooker cooks food at high pressure. Since the container is tightly sealed, the pressure rises easily when the water boils. Once the pressure reaches its maximum, the temperature can go beyond 100°C. And during the peak of this pressure, the valve will release the steam as it cooks. It should be noted that the maximum pressure is 1.8 bar.

The benefits of a pressure cooker

The pressure cooker provides various advantages that must be taken into account:

Ease of use: you will no longer need to check each time if the water has run out or not, since the valve indicates it for you.

Better quality of food: cooking at high temperature allows certain mineral salts contained in food to be retained.

Time saving: it will only take you 30 minutes maximum to cook fairly hard and solid foods.

Adaptation to all types of food: there is no discrimination as to which foods can be cooked or not in a pressure cooker.

The pressure cooker or the traditional pot?

It goes without saying that the pressure cooker is very practical for cooking food quickly and it has many other advantages as well. However, to refine the taste of certain foods, the use of a traditional pot is always an option, although this can be adapted with the pressure cooker.

The pressure cooker or pressure cooker is often used to ensure the quality of cooking in most restaurants these days, but also to not keep customers waiting too long. Compared to the traditional pot, the pressure cooker has several advantages, which really make it stand out. So, you now know what a pressure cooker is, do not hesitate to use one.

Pot au feu

Preparation: 10 minutes   Ready in: 50 min   Portions: 4 people

INGREDIENTS	PREPARATION

INGREDIENTS

- 1 kg meat for stew
- Salt (coarse), pepper
- 2 onions studded with 4 cloves
- 1 clove of garlic
- 2 celery stalks, left whole
- 3 leeks remaining whole
- 3 turnips cut in 4
- 1 kg of carrots cut into pieces
- 1 kg of potatoes
- Water
- Mustard for presentation

PREPARATION

1. Cut the meat into large cubes (or ask the butcher), place them in the bottom of the pressure cooker.
2. Add the water (cold for me) to cover the meat. Salt pepper.
3. Add all the vegetables except the potatoes.
4. Leave to cook for 30 minutes from the turn of the valve.
5. Open the pan (after removing the steam), add the potatoes, peeled and cut into large pieces.
6. Cook again for 15 minutes from the turn of the valve.

Pieces of pure pork and seasonal vegetables

Preparation: 30 mins *Ready in: 30 min* *Portions: 2 people*

INGREDIENTS

- 350-400 g of pure pork,
- Mg,
- 2-3 shallots,
- 1 clove of garlic,
- 2 carrots,
- 2 turnips,
- 200 g of Bx cabbage,
- 1 sprig of thyme,
- 1 bay leaf,
- Salt pepper.

PREPARATION

1. In your pressure cooker, brown the meat over high heat in a knob of butter.
2. Season.
3. When the piece is golden, deglaze with white wine (or beer or water, according to taste), mix to release the juices and reserve the meat.
4. Replace with shallots and garlic, mix and cook for 1 to 2 minutes.
5. ...Then add the vegetables (here pieces of carrots, turnips and Bx cabbage).
6. Season to taste and add the aromatic herbs.
7. Pour about 20 cl of water and cook for about 7-8 minutes over low heat when the pan is under pressure.
8. Check the cooking and seasoning of the vegetables after having opened them, rectify if necessary.

Roasted pork loin in whole milk

Preparation: 30 mins **Ready in: 25 min** **Portions: 4 people**

INGREDIENTS

- 600g of roasted pork loin.
- 600 g medium potatoes.
- 1 large yellow onion
- 3 cloves of garlic.
- 50 cl of milk.
- Olive oil.
- Salt, pepper, thyme, bay leaf, parsley.
- 1 pressure cooker of course.

PREPARATION

1. Peel the onion, garlic and medium potatoes.
2. Cut the onion into four or six segments.
3. Prick the roast with the garlic cloves.
4. In the pressure cooker, brown the filet mignon on each side over high heat in the olive oil.
5. Season with salt and pepper and sprinkle with thyme if desired.
6. Add and sauté the onion.
7. Moisten with milk, put a few crumbs of a bay leaf and close the pressure cooker.
8. When the valve whispers, lower the heat and cook for 10 minutes.
9. Release the steam, open and add the potatoes.
10. When the valve whispers, lower the heat and cook for 12 minutes.
11. Arrange the cut or whole roast in the centre of a plate surrounded by the potatoes, sprinkle with parsley.
12. Pass the sauce from the pressure cooker through a colander, cover the dish and put the rest in a sauce boat.

Marseille packet feet

Preparation: 15 mins   **Ready in: 3 hrs**   **Servings: 6 people**

INGREDIENTS

PREPARATION

- 16 bundles and 16 sheep's feet
- 1 case of 800 g of whole tomatoes
- 1 sugar and 1 pinch of baking soda
- 2 to 3 onions, chopped
- 3 sliced carrots + 1 case chopped garlic/parsley
- 1 bouquet garni (thyme, rosemary, bay leaf, 2 leek leaves, parsley)
- 1/2 liter of dry white wine
- 1/2 liter of water
- • Flower of salt + pepper + Provencal herbs
- Cortex
- Accompaniment
- Serve with garlic and parsley hash browns or baked spirals

1. In the bottom of the pressure cooker, put the rind.
2. Add the stalks, bundles, carrots, tomatoes, onions, wine, water, bouquet garni, Provence herbs, sugar, baking soda and fleur de sel.
3. Leave to cook for 30 minutes uncovered to evaporate the alcohol, then close the pan and cook for 5/6 hours over very low heat from pressurisation. The longer the cooking, the better.
4. After a minimum of 5/6 hours of cooking, preheat the oven to 160°.
5. Run the pressure cooker under cold water to release the steam through the valve. Be careful, it is very hot.
6. Arrange the thighs and the papillotes in a gratin dish with the sauce and the garlic and parsley. Place a sheet of aluminium foil on top and bake for 1 hour. The sauce should thicken a bit.

Pork chops with tomato sauce

Preparation: 1 min   **Ready in:** 30 min   **Portions:** 2 people

INGREDIENTS

PREPARATION

- 2 ribs
- 1 knob of butter
- 1 clove of garlic
- 1 bunch of herbs
- 2 cases of tomato puree
- 1/2 glass of water
- 3 cases of liquid cream
- Salt
- Pepper

1. Brown the onions cut into 4-6 pieces.
2. Add the chops. Let brown.
3. Add the minced garlic and the bouquet garni.
4. Salt pepper.
5. Dilute the tomato with water.
6. Pour into the pressure cooker.
7. As soon as the valve is under pressure, simmer for 8 minutes. on slow fire.
8. Remove and keep ribs warm.
9. Remove the bouquet garni.
10. Add the cream to the sauce.
11. Mix until boiling.
12. Pour over ribs and serve hot.

Fricassee of guinea fowl with peas

Preparation: 15 mins   **Ready in: 23 min**   **Portions : 6 people**

INGREDIENTS

- 6 guinea fowl or chicken legs
- 1 kg frozen peas
- 1 onion
- 20cl of white wine
- 20cl of chicken broth
- 20cl liquid cream
- 1 tablespoon olive oil
- 1 package of smoked bacon

PREPARATION

1. Peel and chop the onion.
2. In your pressure cooker, brown the chicken on all sides for 5 min.
3. Reserve the thighs on a separate plate.
4. In the pressure cooker, pour the oil and sauté the onion for 5 minutes.
5. Then pour in the white wine, simmer for 2-3 minutes, then add the guinea fowl.
6. Mix everything and add the peas, bacon bits and broth, stir everything for 5 minutes, then close the pressure cooker and stop cooking 10 minutes after the start of hissing.
7. Open the pressure cooker after removing the safety seal, add the cream and allow to thicken for another 5 minutes.

Lamb and its vegetables

Preparation : 30 mins　　　**Ready in: 30 min**　　　**Portions : 4 people**

INGREDIENTS

- 30 g of fat (butter or oil),
- 1 onion,
- 800 g lamb shoulder or neck (with some bones),
- 1 Case of flour,
- 1/2 liter of water,
- 2 carrots,
- 1 kg of turnips,
- 1 bunch of herbs,
- 150-200g cooked white beans (Small Case),
- Salt and pepper

PREPARATION

1. In the pressure cooker, with the MG, brown the onion and the meat cut into pieces.
2. Sift the flour over the meat.
3. And add 1/2 liter of water.
4. To mix together.
5. Close the pressure cooker and cook for 10 minutes when the pressure cooker has risen.
6. During this operation, cut the carrots into thin slices (or dice).
7. Add to the pot with the bouquet garni, the small white beans, salt and pepper.
8. Cook over low heat for about fifteen minutes (until the carrots are cooked).
9. Serve the meat with the vegetables.

Turkey Bracarense (Portugal)

Preparation : 30 mins　　　*Ready in: 20 mins*　　*Portions : 6 people*

INGREDIENTS

- 1 large onion
- 3 cloves of garlic
- 60g olive oil
- 1 turkey leg of about 1.5 kg or pieces of chicken
- 1 small case of peeled tomatoes in juice
- 1/2 strong chorizo (about 110g), cut into pieces
- 200g smoked bacon
- 1 chicken stock cube
- 1 bay leaf
- 150 g shredded white cabbage
- 200g frozen peas
- 300 g long cooked rice
- Salt and pepper
- Water

PREPARATION

1. Chop the onion and garlic in a food processor with the olive oil. Put in the pan and brown.
2. Add the meat and brown. Then add the tomatoes, chorizo, bacon, stock cube, bay leaf, salt and pepper, 200 ml of water. Close the pressure cooker and cook for 15 minutes.
3. Remove the meat and set aside.
4. Add the cabbage, peas, rice and 500ml water to the pan. Mix and close the pan for another 15 minutes of cooking.
5. Add water, if necessary, place the meat on the rice and close the lid. Leave on low heat for a few minutes, just long enough to heat the meat. No need to build the pressure cooker. Check that there is enough water so that the rice does not stick to the bottom.
6. In the original recipe there is also chilli, but if my chorizo was strong, it suddenly becomes too spicy. With a mild chorizo, you will need to add a little Espelette pepper.

Bourguignon my way (Provençal style)

Preparation : 30 mins   Ready in: mins   Servings : 4 people

INGREDIENTS	PREPARATION

Cooking time: 2 to 3 hours over low heat so that the meat is very tender or 1 hour in a pressure cooker.

- 1 kg beef bourguignon
- 250g onions
- 300g mushrooms
- 2 cases of chopped tomato pulp
- 1 bottle of bolognese sauce
- 2 beef stock cubes
- 1 bouquet garni cube
- 1 pot of beef heart broth
- 2 cases of oil + 2 cases of olive oil
- 2 teaspoons masala (no spices needed)

1. In a non-stick skillet or your pressure cooker depending on your preference, heat the oil and olive oil. Take the pieces of meat and brown them by adding a little salt and pepper. Once the golden pieces add the onion and the mushrooms as well as the crushed tomatoes, the Bolognese sauce, in short all the other ingredients by adding the equivalent of two pots of tomato pulp in the water.

2. Let simmer for the time required according to the meat cooking method chosen. You can accompany this dish with potatoes cut in 4, boiled and cooked in the juice of the dish at the end of cooking, or with pasta or potatoes, or even with the rest in the evening or the next day, combine the beans greens in the dish with meat sauce

Yves' Stew

Preparation : 15 mins   **Servings : 4 people**

INGREDIENTS

- 1kg of beef (in the: Shank, Gite, Paleron, Osso Bucco etc.)
- 1 marrow, a slice of salted duck breast (*especially not smoked),
- 1Kg of Carrots
- 1 Liter of wine (White, Red, Rosé)
- 1 onion sprinkled with a dozen cloves
- 1 orange zest
- 1 square of dark chocolate
- 125g of black olives
- 4 garlic cloves, salt
- Ground pepper
- 1 bouquet garni, 2-3 tablespoons cognac
- 1 leek (*optional)

PREPARATION

1. The day before; In a large saucepan, marinate the meat with all the ingredients indicated.
2. The same day; In the same pot (cast iron is better) cook everything over low heat for as long as possible (6 or even 8 hours) when the liquid level has halved, add the same amount of water or broth beef and let reduce as much as possible.
3. For binding; I do it without flour! Mine is more than better!
4. In a "blister" or "soup mixer" pour the olives, the garlic cloves without skin, the orange zest and the onion detached from its teeth, a little broth then mix everything until obtaining a smooth cream that you add to the whole.

Provencal squid breast

Preparation : 15 mins   Ready in : 5 to 10 min   Servings : 4 people

INGREDIENTS

- 500g cuttlefish whites
- 1 or 2 tablespoons of olive oil
- 1 chopped onion
- 4 tomatoes or coulis
- 2 cloves garlic
- ¼ liter dry white wine
- 1 tbsp parsley
- Salt
- Pepper

PREPARATION

1. Cut the cuttlefish into strips, brown them with the onion in the pressure cooker with 1 or 2 tablespoons of oil.

2. After a few minutes, add the tomatoes (or the coulis), the bouquet garni, the minced garlic cloves, salt and pepper. Moisten with white wine. Bring to a boil, then close the pressure cooker. Cook over low heat for 10 minutes from the pressure setting.

3. Accompanying the cuttlefish whites with white rice, adding a few tablespoons of fresh cream at the end does not take anything away, quite the contrary.

Easy couscous

INGREDIENTS

- 8 chicken thighs
- 12 Merguez
- 500g lamb
- Olive oil
- 2 cases of tomato puree
- 3 tablespoons of couscous spices
- 1 teaspoon of harissa
- 2 beef stock cubes
- 3 large tomatoes
- 10 small turnips
- 6 carrots
- 2 zucchinis
- 1 box of chickpeas

PREPARATION

1. Wash and peel the carrots, turnips and tomatoes and cut them into cubes.
2. In your pressure cooker, pour 3 tablespoons of olive oil. Bring to the fire and brown the chicken and lamb. When they are golden brown, pour the equivalent of a liter of water and add the beef stock cubes, tomato puree, carrots, turnips and tomatoes, spiced couscous and harissa. Close the pressure cooker and count 25 minutes of cooking once the pressure rises.
3. Meanwhile, wash and cut the courgettes into cubes and drain the chickpeas.
4. After 25 minutes, remove the steam from your pressure cooker, open and add the zucchini and chickpeas.
5. Put back on the heat and cook the merguez separately in a pan or on the grill.
6. Prepare a fine semolina to accompany: Put the semolina in a bowl, cover with salted water and wait 5 minutes. Then place the bowl for 2 minutes in the microwave with a piece of butter. Using a fork, remove the couscous grains.

Sautéed hunter's veal

Preparation : 15 mins   *Ready in: 2 hrs*   *Servings : 6 people*

INGREDIENTS

- 1 kg 700 "Dew of the Pyrenees" veal sauté

For me blanquette and pieces on the bone

- 500g of mushrooms

For me frozen

- 4 shallots
- 7 carrots
- 6 tomatoes
- 2 glasses of dry white wine
- 1 tablespoon of tomato puree
- 2 tablespoons olive oil
- 2 cloves garlic
- Basil, parsley, chopped
- Salt
- Pepper

PREPARATION

1. Pour the oil into the pan or pressure cooker and brown the meat cut into pieces.
2. until golden brown on all sides.
3. Add the peeled and chopped shallots, the peeled and chopped carrots.
4. Diced tomatoes, frozen mushrooms,
5. White wine, peeled and chopped garlic, herbs, seasoning.
6. Cover and simmer for about 1h30 over low heat or in a pressure cooker; then the time will be reduced, count 30 minutes from the rotation of the valve.
7. Note that there is no sauce and the meat is very tender.

Duck leg

Preparation : 3 h   Ready in: 2 hrs   Servings : 6 people

INGREDIENTS

- 1.5 kg of duck
- 750g chorizo meat
- 1 carrot
- 2 onions
- 1 bunch of herbs
- 1 clove of garlic
- 1 egg
- 5 cl cognac
- 10 gr of salt and 3 gr of pepper per kilo

PREPARATION

1. Bone the duck.
2. Make a jus with the bones by browning them in the fat with 1 carrot and 1 chopped onion. Add 1 liter of cold water, the bouquet garni and the garlic. Leave to cook for 1 hour, filter the broth and reduce the juice to around 20 cl.
3. Chop the meat with 1 onion, 5 cl of cognac, 20 cl of juice, salt, pepper and egg. Cook in a terrine, garnished with fatty or smoked bacon, for 1 hour at 180° OR in small terrines or jars with 1 bay leaf in each puff pastry and sterilize for 3 hours at 100° in your pressure cooker.

Shepherd's pie with Swiss chard

Preparation : 45 mins   **Ready in: 30 min**   **Portions : 8 people**

INGREDIENTS

- 100 g of St Morêt (for the chard)
- 1 large onion
- 500g minced pork
- 300g ground beef
- 1 kg 500 Monalisa potatoes
- 50 g semi-salted butter or oil (for the mash)
- 30g grated cheese
- Olive oil
- Salt pepper,

PREPARATION

1. Start by cleaning your chard, separating the ribs and keeping only the green, the leaves.
2. Rinse thoroughly, then cook in salted water in your pressure cooker, drain and set aside.
3. Peel the potatoes, cut them into large pieces and also cook them in salted water and in a pressure cooker; then pass through a grinder, add a little cooking water if necessary, season with pepper, add semi-salted butter or oil and set aside.
4. In a sauté pan, pour 1 tablespoon of olive oil then brown, but not too much, the finely chopped onion; it should not burn add ½ glass of water until the water is completely absorbed, salt, pepper, also set aside.
5. In the same frying pan pour 1 tablespoon of olive oil, add the 2 minced meats and colour by shelling with a fork, season if the meat is smooth, set aside.
6. Still in the pan; add the chard, salt and pepper, if necessary, add the St Morêt, mix well and set aside.
7. Preheat the oven to 200°.
8. In a large gratin dish, spread the onion layer on the bottom, then half the mashed potatoes, add the pork and the veal, smooth well, then the Swiss chard with St Morêt; finish with the last layer of mashed potatoes,
9. Sprinkle with grated cheese and bake until golden, depending on the oven, about 30 minutes.
10. If it is a Pyrex dish, you can serve the Parmenter directly at the table, otherwise.
11. On an individual plate using a cookie cutter (to be made the day before) and reheat.

Thai fried rice with shrimp paste and caramelized pork

Preparation : 45 mins   *Servings : 2 people*

INGREDIENTS

PREPARATION

For the fried rice:
- 2 bowls of cooked rice (preferably pressure cooker)
- 2 tablespoons olive oil
- 1 tablespoon of shrimp paste
- 1 finely chopped shallot
- 1 clove garlic finely chopped
- 1 tablespoon nuoc Nam

For the caramelized pork:
- 200g pork (ham)
- 3 tablespoons of sugar
- 1 tablespoon cider vinegar
- 1 clove garlic finely chopped
- 2 tablespoons olive oil
- Pepper

For the accompaniment:
- 1 shallot, chopped
- 1 hard mango or Granny Smith apple, julienned
- 2 slices of lime
- 1 egg

1. In a bowl, combine sugar, vinegar, garlic and pepper. Marinate the meat for at least 1 hour (ideally: overnight). In a deep saucepan, pour the marinade with the meat, ½ glass of water and boil until the liquid evaporates. Add the olive oil and brown the pork. Cut into small pieces and set aside.
2. Prepare the filling:
3. Slice the shallot, cut the mango into julienne strips, make a thin omelette with the egg and cut it into strips.
4. Prepare the fried rice:
5. In a wok or skillet pour the olive oil, chilli, garlic and shrimp paste. Fry then add the 2 bowls of cooked rice. Fry while stirring and season with nuoc Nam.
6. Serve each bowl of this fried rice with a wedge of lime, shallot, mango, caramelized pork and tortilla.

Parmenter with pumpkin

Preparation : 15 mins   *Ready in: 25 min*   *Portions : 4 people*

INGREDIENTS

- Olive oil
- 1 large onion, chopped
- 400g ground beef
- 10 cl of tomato coulis
- 1 tablespoon paprika
- 1 sprig of thyme
- 4 potatoes
- 1 pumpkin
- grated cheese
- Salt
- Pepper

PREPARATION

1. Preheat the oven to 200°C. In a skillet, heat the oil and brown the onion. Add the meat and brown for a few minutes. Add the tomato coulis, paprika and thyme. Season with salt and pepper and continue cooking for 5 minutes over low heat.
2. Cut the pumpkin into quarters and take 500 g of pulp. Peel the potatoes, and cut them into pieces. Cook the squash and potatoes together in your pressure cooker. Drain and pass through a potato masher. Salt and pepper.
3. In a gratin dish, pour the contents of the pan. Garnish with mashed potatoes/pumpkin. Sprinkle with grated cheese. Bake for 15 minutes in the oven.

Liège salad (potatoes and green beans)

Preparation : 30 mins   **Ready in: 30 min**   **Portions : 2 people**

INGREDIENTS

- 250 g firm-fleshed potato
- 300 g green beans (princesses), whole or cut in 2-3,
- 150 g pork belly, pancetta, fresh, SMOKED (for me), ...
- 1 chopped shallot,
- 1 chopped onion,
- 2-3 cases of wine vinegar, RASPBERRY vinegar (for me), ...
- 1 Case of lard, or butter,
- Chopped flat-leaf parsley (1 tablespoon),
- Salt pepper

PREPARATION

1. Wash, cook the potatoes in a pan of salted boiling water.
2. Wash and peel the beans. Cook them in a pan of boiling water for 5 to 10 minutes.
3. They must stand firm.
4. For my part, I cook the potatoes cut into pieces and the beans together, steamed,
5. In your pressure cooker, 8-10 minutes, in salted water... Or in water (according to choose).
6. Meanwhile, cut the bacon into small lardons.
7. Fry the bacon in a frying pan over fairly high heat... let it melt.
8. Drain potatoes and beans.
9. Put the potatoes in a bowl and add the beans.
10. In the same skillet, melt the lard/butter in a skillet over medium heat.
11. Add the chopped shallot and onion to the pan, brown.
12. Deglaze with wine or raspberry vinegar.
13. Leave to heat, stirring the vinegar so that it releases all the cooking juices.
14. Salt and pepper to taste.
15. Pour bacon and sauce over potatoes and beans.
16. Sprinkle everything with chopped parsley.
17. Serve hot.
18. A little more... add a little liquid cream.

Pork tenderloin... maroilles sauce and fondant potatoes

Preparation : 30 mins   **Ready in: 15 min**   **Portions : 4 people**

INGREDIENTS

- 2 pork loins of 825 g
- 250ml water
- 100ml white wine
- 2 jars of vegetable broth
- 400 ml 18% semi-thick cream
- 250g Maroilles
- 1 pinch of Espelette pepper
- 1 pinch of 5-berry pepper
- 1 teaspoon thyme leaves
- 300 g of potatoes with almonds
- 3 elongated shallots

PREPARATION

1. Heat the pressure cooker with olive oil. Brown the filet mignon, cut into medallions. Add the chopped shallots, brown them... Five-berry pepper. Espelette pepper. Pour the white wine.
2. Let cook over low heat for 5 minutes.
3. Prepare and return the potatoes cut into pieces in the preparation.
4. Add the water... The pots of vegetable stock...wait for it to boil then add the semi-thick cream...
5. Remove the coloured part of the cheese and scrape it with a knife... Make slices... Reserve 4 for the vinaigrette... 1 slice per plate and cut the slices into pieces and place them in the preparation... Mix...
6. Cook in your pressure cooker for 15 minutes from boiling... Once the preparation is cooked, let the sauce reduce for a good 5 minutes and without waiting...
7. The dish is ready when the sauce is smooth.
8. Accompany each dish with a slice of maroilles... To be enjoyed hot...

Lamb shank with honey, thyme and rosemary

Preparation : 30 mins   **Ready in: 3 hrs**   **Servings : 1 person**

INGREDIENTS

PREPARATION

- 1 lamb shank
- Olive oil
- 2 cases of honey (for me acacia honey)
- 1 clove of garlic
- flower of salt
- Ground pepper
- Thyme (1-2 sprigs)
- Rosemary (1 sprig)
- 1 onion
- 1 good carrot
- 10 cl of white wine
- 10 cl of beef broth
- 1 clove of garlic
- 150 g of Crone de Gate potato

1. In a saucepan, mix and heat 2 cases of oil + 2 cases of honey to obtain a syrup.
2. Over high heat, brown the leg of lamb on all sides in a pan with a drizzle of olive oil (in a pressure cooker for me).
3. Reduce the heat source.
4. Season with Flower of salt and ground pepper.
5. Add the garlic clove, thyme, rosemary, chopped onion.
6. Pour over the honey oil syrup.
7. Cover the pan and simmer for 30 minutes, turning the meat regularly on all sides.
8. Deglaze with white wine.
9. Mix well to collect the cooking juices.
10. Add water and/or beef broth (up to +- half).
11. Cook, covered, for 1h30 (30 min in the pressure cooker).
12. Then add the garlic on your shirt, the carrot slices and the Crone de Gate potato.
13. Continue cooking slowly for about 30 minutes (the carrots and potatoes should be well cooked and the meat should fall easily from the bones).

Chicken with White Wine

Preparation : 30 mins   **Ready in : 2 hrs 30 mins**   **Portions : 4 people**

INGREDIENTS

- 1 free-range rooster, around 1.5 to 1.6 kg
- 200-250g mushrooms
- 100g butter (50+50)
- 1 dl liquid cream
- 3 cases of flour
- 1 onion
- 2-3 shallots
- 3 dl of white wine
- 1 dl cognac
- 1 small bunch of parsley
- Oil
- Salt
- Pepper

PREPARATION

1. Cut out the rooster.
2. Peel, chop the onion and the shallots.
3. In a skillet, brown the pieces of meat in a little oil + half the butter.
4. Brown them all over.
5. Season.
6. Add chopped onions and shallots.
7. Mix well and let brown.
8. Flambé with cognac.
9. Add mushrooms and white wine.
10. Cook over low heat for about 1h30…. About 30 min in the pressure cooker.
11. Add a little water if the juice is not enough.
12. When the chicken is cooked, keep the pieces warm.
13. Mix the rest of the softened butter with the flour, + the cream.
14. Add a little cooking juice to soften the preparation.
15. Pour into the saucepan.
16. Let reduce to a low boil.
17. Return the chicken pieces to the juice.
18. Adjust the seasoning if necessary.
19. Serve hot, sprinkled with chopped parsley, with mashed potatoes, rice, pasta…

Lentils in sauce (Lards)

Preparation : 45 mins   **Ready in: 5 to 10 min**   **Servings : 6 people**

INGREDIENTS

- A few pieces of meat
- 450g green lentils
- 2 onions
- 3 carrots
- 3 tablespoons oil
- 1 tablespoon of Cosbor (homemade spice made from garlic and coriander powder) you can replace it with coriander powder and garlic
- 1 teaspoon paprika
- 1 teaspoon tomato puree

PREPARATION

1. Start by grating the onions, put them in the pressure cooker with the oil and cut the meat into large pieces. Then add all the spices and cover with water (about 1.5 litters). Close the pressure cooker and cook for 5 minutes as soon as the pressure cooker whistles.

2. Meanwhile, peel and cut the carrots into pieces. Open the pressure cooker and add the carrots and lentils. Close the pressure cooker for 5/7 minutes.

3. He is ready! If when opening you notice that there is not enough sauce, add and bring to the boil for a few minutes.

Tagine white beans

Preparation : 1 hour   **Servings : 4 people**

INGREDIENTS

- 1 Bowl of dried white beans previously soaked and puffed in water
- chopped onion
- 4 garlic cloves
- Olive oil
- 1 good grated tomato
- Coriander
- Salt pepper
- ginger paprika
- 8 grilled sausages

PREPARATION

1. Brown everything in your pressure cooker... Add the water... Let it cook... When cooking adds the grilled merguez... Harissa if you like it spicy... C super good. That's my favourite meal...

Brucolac soup

INGREDIENTS

- 1 large red onion
- 200g green lentils
- 1 small case of tomato purée
- 2 cloves garlic
- 1 piece of butter
- 1 squeeze of lemon
- 1 pinch of saffron
- 1 small sweet pepper
- 1 dash of olive oil
- Thyme, bay leaf
- Salt and pepper

PREPARATION

1. Cut the onion into small strips and brown it in a pan with the crushed garlic and butter. Add the tomato paste. Cover everything with 1.5 litters of water.
2. Add the lentils, chilli, saffron, thyme and bay leaf. Salt and pepper. Simmer for 40 minutes (or 20 minutes in a pressure cooker).
3. Remove the pepper. Add a drizzle of lemon and a drizzle of olive oil.
4. Serve with slices of toasted bread rubbed with garlic.

Skillet Bulgur with Chicken and Asparagus

Preparation : 30 mins   **Ready in : 15 min**   **Portions : 4 people**

INGREDIENTS

- 1 glass of bulgur, about 220 g
- Chicken breast 220gr
- White wine 100ml
- 2 red onions
- Guarantee salt, Espelette pepper, Ground pepper
- Frozen green asparagus 100gr
- 2 tablespoons olive oil + butter

PREPARATION

1. Bring 1 liter of salted water to a boil, pour in the bulgur, simmer for 12 minutes, stirring occasionally.
2. Steam the asparagus for 4 minutes in the pressure cooker.
3. Meanwhile, chop the chicken breasts, brown them with a little olive oil and a knob of butter and season with a pinch of Espelette pepper + Guarantee salt + pepper, pour in the white wine and cook over low heat for 8-10 minutes.
4. Add the bulgur green asparagus cut in half beforehand (the remaining stalks will be used for a small starter).
5. Gently mix all your preparation while continuing to cook over very low heat for 2 to 3 minutes.
6. Arrange and sprinkle with strips of raw red onions and asparagus.
7. Enjoy it now...... And I wish you all a good appetite.

Doe steaks with porcini mushrooms and mashed sweet potatoes

Preparation : 30 mins   Ready in: 30 min   Portions : 4 people

INGREDIENTS

- 4 deer fillets
- 2 nice sweet potatoes
- 1 cassolette of 320 g ceps
- 1 good tablespoon of fresh cream
- 1 good piece of butter
- Parsley
- Butter
- Oil

Sauce:
- 20 cl of red wine (Bordeaux)
- 1 good tablespoon of beef broth
- 1 small glass of water
- 1 bunch of herbs
- 1 sugar cube
- 1 tablespoon strawberry jam
- Salt and pepper
- 30g butter

PREPARATION

1. Prepare the mash. Peel and cut the sweet potatoes into chunks. Steam in your pressure cooker for 15 minutes. Then mix them and add the cream and butter. Salt and pepper. Hold You can reheat when ready to serve.
2. Prepare the sauce. In a saucepan, put the wine, the veal stock, 1 small glass of water, the sugar, the bouquet garni and bring to the boil. Reduce by half over low heat. Season with salt and pepper, remove the bouquet garni. Add the strawberry jam and mix well. Beat the butter, cut it into small pieces and set aside, heat.
3. Cook the meat in olive oil for 5 minutes on each side. It should be pink. Salt and pepper.
4. Drain and rinse the porcini pieces. Then put them in olive oil for at least 5 minutes. Add chopped parsley. Salt and pepper.
5. Serve hot, accompanied by cannons.

Endives with prawns

Preparation : 15 mins   **Ready in : 15 min**   **Portions : 2 people**

INGREDIENTS

- 4 chicories
- 10 large cooked prawns or "branches"
- Lemon juice
- 1 vegetable broth diluted in 20 cl of very hot water
- 10 cl heavy cream
- Chopped chives
- Salt pepper

PREPARATION

1. Clean, remove the base and the heart of the endives, place them in the basket of the pressure cooker containing the vegetable broth, salt and pepper and sprinkle with lemon juice. Close the pressure cooker, expect to cook for fifteen minutes as soon as the valve whispers.
2. Shell the prawns.
3. In a saucepan, heat the sour cream over low heat with about ten tablespoons of broth recovered from the pressure cooker, salt and pepper. When the mixture is hot, remove from the heat, add the shrimp.
4. Arrange the endives cut into pieces in pretty bowls, drizzle with shrimp sauce and sprinkle with chives.

Sterilization of candied tomatoes

INGREDIENTS

- 2 sprigs of thyme
- 1 bay leaf
- 2-3 garlic cloves
- Salt
- Pepper
- 4-5 Cases of sugar
- Olive oil

PREPARATION

1. And dry the tomatoes.
2. Put them in a saucepan.
3. Add the thyme, bay leaf and garlic cloves (cleaned and cut into 4).
4. Salt pepper.
5. Add the sugar.
6. Drizzle generously with olive oil.
7. Cook for about 30 minutes over medium heat, covered, stirring occasionally.
PRESSURE COOKER STERILIZATION.
8. The valve should barely whisper to maintain the pressure at 100°.
9. Fill the pressure cooker 1/3 full with water.
10. Place a kitchen towel in the bottom of the pan and between the jars (to prevent the jars from bumping into each other and bumping into the bottom while cooking).
11. Close the lid and pressurize.
12. Count about 40-50 minutes of sterilization by barely whispering the valve.
13. When cooking is complete, leave the soup, do not remove the steam.
14. The pressure should drop on its own,
15. The pan must be completely cooled before opening it.
16. When it's cold, check the tightness of the jars by trying to open them without forcing too much.
17. Well cooled, wash the jars.

Khlii express

Preparation : h   **Ready in: 1 hr**   **Servings: 8 people**

INGREDIENTS	PREPARATION

INGREDIENTS

- 1 kg meat, cut into 4 cm wide strips
- 1 Bowl of beef or lamb fat. . . Cut into small pieces
- 1 bowl of olive oil
- 1 heaped teaspoon of salt
- 1 glass of vinegar tea
- 1 tablespoon ground cumin
- 2 tablespoons coriander seeds, finely ground
- 5 whole heads of garlic
- 1/2 liter of water

PREPARATION

1. Mix the garlic add the vinegar, salt, cumin and coriander. Wash the meat, drain it and add the marinade. Leave to macerate overnight in the refrigerator....

2. Put the beef fat and water in the pressure cooker, bring to a boil before adding the meat. Leave to cook for one hour. Remove the meat and cook over low heat until the water has completely evaporated.

3. The meat should brown... and become a little crispy...

4. Leave to cool and preferably put in a glass jar. The express Khlii can be kept for fifteen days to a month because the meat has not been dried in the sun like the classic Khlii....

5. Each time you want to add it to a preparation, you take out its precious jar... And equipped with scissors, you cut as many pieces as you want... You put it back in the fridge...

Beef tagine with prunes and sesame seeds

Preparation : 1 hr 30 mins   **Ready in : 1 h 40 min**   **Portions : 6 people**

INGREDIENTS

PREPARATION

- 1kg of beef
- 3 onions
- 1 tomato
- 1 small bunch of parsley and coriander
- 1 cinnamon stick
- 2 cases of olive oil
- 1 teaspoon of salt 1 teaspoon of pepper
- 1 teaspoon paprika
- 1 teaspoon of turmeric
- 1/2 tsp raz el hanut
- 1/2 teaspoon ground cinnamon

For the prunes
- 200g prunes
- 50g caster sugar
- 50g of butter
- 1/2 teaspoon ground cinnamon
- 50g sesame seeds

1. In a pot, brown your meat with olive oil, add the onions, brown, mix well and scrape their juices from the bottom of the pot. Add a glass of water, your spices, parsley and coriander. Cook for half an hour and add your diced tomatoes. Continue cooking, the meat should be tender or tender. You can use your pressure cooker, but be careful not to drown your meat, you will lose all the flavours. Count a good hour of cooking. When the meat is cooked, remove it from the pan and keep it warm.

2. In the pot, pour your prunes with sugar, butter and cinnamon, add water if necessary. Simmer until a smooth and creamy sauce is obtained. At this point, put the meat back and simmer another 10 minutes to a quarter of an hour.

3. Serve on a large plate, placing the meat on top with the prunes sprinkled with sesame seeds and the sauce below that makes this dish such a success.

Tripe with Paimpol beans

Preparation : 15 mins   **Ready in : 1 hr 30 min**   **Servings : 6 people**

INGREDIENTS

- Guts
- 1 piece of lung (optional)
- 800g peeled Paimpol beans
- 2 garlic cloves, minced
- Parsley, coriander
- 1 chopped onion
- 2 teaspoons of paprika
- 1 teaspoon of ginger
- ½ teaspoon cumin
- ½ teaspoon smen (optional)
- 1 teaspoon of turmeric
- A pinch of cinnamon and food colouring
- Salt pepper
- A pinch of harissa (to taste)
- 2 to 3 tablespoons of olive oil
- 2 tomatoes cut into pieces
- 2 teaspoons of tomato puree (depending on the desired colour)
- A bay leaf's
- A little water

PREPARATION

1. During Mutton Festival, we always chop (liver, heart, kidney, lung and tripe together).
2. I hadn't cooked the tripe yet, so here's the recipe. This year I made them with white beans, otherwise we made them with carrots and potatoes.
3. Blanch the tripe, drain, rinse and cut into pieces.
4. In your pressure cooker we put the tripe and all the other ingredients except the beans. Cover with water and cook over low heat for about 1h30.
5. Meanwhile, pre-cook the beans for about 20 minutes in hot, unsalted water to prevent them from hardening. You can use dried white beans but you must let them swell for 12 hours in cold water.
6. After 1h30, check the cooking of the tripe, add the beans, adjust the seasoning and cook again in the closed pan for 15 minutes until the beans and the tripe are tender.

Picardy wild ducks with turnips

Preparation : 30 mins   *Ready in : 1 hr*   *Servings : 4 people*

INGREDIENTS	PREPARATION

INGREDIENTS

- 2 small ducks (blue-green breed) of 500 gr
- 1 large red onion
- 4 turnip balls
- 2 large rutabagas
- Salt + Espelette pepper
- Thyme pepper + 1 sprig of rosemary + bay leaf powder
- 500ml chicken stock
- 250ml white wine
- 1 tablespoon of olive oil + 1 large knob of butter
- 1 sugar cube

PREPARATION

1. Wash and cut the vegetables into cubes.
2. Gently brown the ducks in the olive oil and thyme and rosemary butter, season and remove the ducks.
3. Melt the onion, put the ducks back, first fill half a turnip cut into cubes in each of them, drizzle with white wine and cook over low heat for 5 minutes, pour the 500 ml of broth.
4. Cook gently in your pressure cooker for 40 minutes depending on the weight of the ducks!
5. Now add the turnips, sugar, Espelette pepper, cook over low heat for 20 minutes.

Endive gratin from Picardy with Reblochon cheese and Emmental cheese

INGREDIENTS	PREPARATION

INGREDIENTS

- 8 large ground endives + 2 (from my Somme region in Picardy)
- 4 litters of ham
- 4 Strasbourg sausages
- 1 Reblochon cheese of 240g
- 1 cubed chicken
- 2 small yellow onions
- 2 shallots
- 2 cloves garlic
- 20g butter + pepper

Béchamel sauce:
- 50g butter
- 50g flour
- 25 cl of liquid cream at 30
- 500ml endive broth
- 1 teaspoon powdered sugar + pepper + nutmeg

PREPARATION

1. Start by peeling the leaves of the 2 endives and removing part of the trunk of the other endives, leaving them whole.
2. Cut the onions into strips, chopped shallots and crush the peeled garlic.
3. Heat your pressure cooker put your knob of butter melt your onions, shallots and garlic do not brown then the escarole leaves and the whole ones. Add chicken broth and pepper. Simmer for 15 minutes in your pressure cooker.
4. Once cooked, drain the leaves and separate the endives, collect the endive broth which will be used for the béchamel.
5. Prepare your bechamel butter + flour + endive broth + sugar + liquid cream + nutmeg + pepper.
6. Place the escarole leaves on your plate, cover with a little bechamel sauce, place the 4 endives, wrap them in ham and the 4 others, put a sausage inside.
7. Cover with the rest of the béchamel sauce, slice 8 slices of Reblochon, place on each escarole and sprinkle with Gruyere Emmental.
8. Bake in preheated oven at 180 degrees.

winter pumpkin soup

Preparation : 30 mins   **Ready in : 15 min**   **Portions : 4 people**

INGREDIENTS

- 1 good slice of pumpkin
- 1 white leek
- 1 carrot
- 1 onion
- 1 clove of garlic
- 1 liter of chicken broth
- Salt pepper).

PREPARATION

1. Cut the vegetables into large chunks.
2. Let the onion and garlic sweat for a few moments in a little fat.
3. Add chopped vegetables.
4. Season with pepper.
5. Cover with chicken broth.
6. Mixer.
7. Reseason if necessary.
8. Served with toasted bread dippers (I prefer to dip the bread as I go than let the bread soak).
9. A few strips of freshly cut and caught mushrooms, raw... It's great!!
10. A little spicier? A turn of the pepper mill, paprika, chilli... To taste.
11. A cloud of hot milk or cream if, on the contrary, you want more sweetness!

Green bean salad, bacon, potato, new onion vinaigrette

Preparation : 30 mins　　　**Ready in : 30 min**　　　**Portions : 1 person**

INGREDIENTS

- 1 good big handful of green beans
- 2 small potatoes
- 1 egg
- Smoked bacon (+-75g)
- 1 shallot
- Parsley

In the dressing:

- 2 spring onions
- 1 teaspoon of mustard
- 2 cases of wine vinegar
- 4 cans of rapeseed oil

PREPARATION

1. Clean the green beans, cut them into 2-3 parts.
2. Cook the potatoes in lightly salted boiling water.
3. Beans cooked on top, in the steamer basket.
4. For me, 10 min in the pressure cooker.
5. Cook the egg for 9 minutes in water (boiled egg).
6. Pass it under cold water, peel it.
7. Cut the bacon into thin sticks.
8. Wash and chop the parsley.
9. Cut the spring onions into thin rings.
10. Combine the dressing ingredients:
11. Spring onions, mustard, vinegar and oil.
12. Sweat the bacon, add the chopped shallot. To mix together.
13. Add beans, cut potatoes (according to size).
14. Pepper (the bacon is already salty).
15. Mix everything gently.
16. Served on the plate.
17. Dressing is poured over it.
18. Decorate with the hard-boiled egg cut in 4 and the parsley.

Steamed cod papillote

Preparation : 30 mins   *Ready in : 10 mins*   *Portions : 4 people*

INGREDIENTS

PREPARATION

- 1 frozen cod fillet still frozen,
- 1/3 to 1/2 tomato cut into quarters,
- 2 pinches of chopped parsley leaves,
- A drizzle of olive oil
- Salt pepper
- And, if desired, a pinch of fennel seeds

1. Arrange the cod back, the tomatoes, the parsley on aluminium foil.
2. Drizzle with olive oil, salt, pepper and sprinkle with fennel seeds.
3. Close the sheet.
4. Pour 2 to 3 cm of water into the bottom of the pressure cooker.
5. Put the papillotes in the basket, lower the heat by turning the valve and cook for 20 minutes (frozen fish) or 10 minutes (fresh fish).
6. The papillotes can be served with steamed potatoes (which can be cooked at the same time as the fish in the pressure cooker basket: hence the use of still frozen fish to harmonize cooking times) or with white rice cooked separately.

Old fashioned veal stew

Preparation : 45 mins   *Servings : 6 people*

INGREDIENTS	PREPARATION

INGREDIENTS

- 2 kg of beef:
- Piece of blanquette on the shoulder,
- Tendrons and 1 braised veal
- 2 carrots
- 2 onions
- 240 g canned mushrooms
- 1 kilo of potatoes (charlotte or pompadour)
- 40g of butter
- 4 tablespoons of flour
- 1 liter of hot water
- 1 bunch of herbs
- 2 nails
- Salt pepper

For the binding

- 2 egg yolks
- 3 tablespoons fresh cream
- 1 lemon juice

PREPARATION

1. In the pressure cooker, brown all the meat cut into large cubes and the braised veal in the butter.
2. Do not put the bone with the marrow, set aside.
3. Add the sliced carrots and chopped onions, when everything is nicely browned add the flour and boiling water until the meat is covered, season with salt and pepper.
4. Put the bouquet garni and the cloves, close and count 25 minutes from the pressurization,
5. Open the pressure cooker, remove the bouquet garni, add the marrow, the potatoes cut into large slices
6. Check the seasoning of the drained mushrooms and add the rest of the still boiling water if necessary.
7. Give maximum 25 minutes it's ready.
8. Now we need to prepare the connection:
9. In a terrine, melt the egg yolks and the fresh cream, add one or two ladles of juice, the lemon juice, mix everything, pour into the veal blanquette, place in the dish and serve immediately.
10. The potatoes are sublime, tender.

Rack of pork with rosemary and pastis

Preparation : 15 mins   **Servings : 4 people**

INGREDIENTS

- 1 roast suckling pig (1-1,200 kg), bone-in,
- 1 shallot,
- 1 clove of garlic,
- 1 knob of butter + 1 tablespoon of oil,
- 1 sprig of rosemary,
- 1 bay leaf,
- 10-20cl of Pastis,
- Salt pepper
- Small courgettes (green and yellow)
- Leftover ratatouille and peppers.

PREPARATION

1. I cooked this roast in a pressure cooker (multiply the cooking time by 3 for a classic casserole).
2. Cut the meat.
3. Remove the bones (reserve them).
4. Brown it on all sides in the pressure cooker in a knob of butter + a drizzle of oil, as well as the bones.
5. Add the finely chopped shallot and the lightly crushed clove of garlic.
6. Season with salt, pepper.
7. Deglaze with the pastis.
8. Rub the bottom of the pan well to collect the juice.
9. Add a background of water (wine, beer, etc.).
10. Add the sprig of rosemary and the bay leaf.
11. Then at the top, in the steam basket, thinly sliced zucchini (I alternated the 2 colours).
12. Season.
13. Close the pressure cooker and cook for 8 minutes when the valve is under pressure.
14. Cut the meat into thin slices.
15. Serve (cold or hot), with a little cooking juice.

Katsudon *Japanese*

Preparation : 15 mins   **Ready in : 05 min**   **Portions : 1 person**

INGREDIENTS

- 1 thin slice of pork (boneless loin)
- 1 egg
- 1 onion
- 65ml water
- 2 tablespoons of soy sauce
- 2 tablespoons hon mirin
- 1/2 teaspoon dashi
- 1 teaspoon of sugar
- Panko (Japanese breadcrumbs)
- Rice for 1 pers. cooked (preferably in your pressure cooker)
- Salt and pepper
- Frying oil and a little flour

PREPARATION

1. Slice the onion and put it in a pan with soy + water + sugar + hon mirin + dashi.
2. Cover your pan and cook for a few minutes over medium heat, until the onion is tender, then remove the pan from the heat.
3. Meanwhile, give your meat a few stabs, salt and pepper.
4. Beat your egg, add a drop of water and separate it in half (one part will be used for the breadcrumbs).
5. Take your meat, coat it in flour, then dip it in egg, then top it with panko and fry it.
6. Once the meat is cooked, drain it for a few minutes then cut it into fairly thin pieces.
7. Put it in the sauce with the onion and the rest of the egg and cover for two or three minutes over medium-low heat so that the sauce soaks the meat well.
8. Serve over hot rice!

Oyakodon or Tanindon *Japanese*

Preparation : 15 mins   *Servings : 1 person*

INGREDIENTS

- 75 g minced pork or chicken (or finely minced)
- 1/2 Onion
- 1 egg
- 1/2 teaspoon of dashi,
- 1cc Sugar
- 1 to 2 tablespoons of soy sauce
- 60ml water
- 1 bowl of rice (cooked in a pressure cooker or steamed)

PREPARATION

1. Finely chop the onion and only use half of it!
2. In a pot:
   Put the water + the dashi + the sugar + the onion to cook (cover).
   When the onion is half-cooked: add the meat (pork or chicken) and the soy sauce. Mix well and cover.
   Once the meat is almost cooked: add the egg (previously beaten!!) and cover again.
3. As soon as the egg seems cooked, serve it on a bowl of hot rice and enjoy...
4. You can add chives, shichimi to decorate.

Oxtail salad

Preparation : 3 h   **Ready in: 7 h**   **Portions : 4 people**

INGREDIENTS

PREPARATION

- 1 oxtail
- 1 bunch of herbs
- 1 beef stock cube
- 1 tablespoon of coarse salt according to your taste
- Pepper
- 2 carrots
- 1 kg potato
- 2 onions
- 3 tablespoons old wine vinegar
- 8 tablespoons of sunflower oil
- Parsley
- Fine salt

1. In a pressure cooker put the oxtail, the bouquet garni, the sliced carrots, the coarse salt, the stock in cubes. Cover with water and cook for 3 hours according to the traditional method.
2. Cook the potatoes in their jackets. Then peel them and set them aside.
3. Drain the meat, reserve the carrots.
4. Peel the oxtail.
5. In a bowl, put the oxtail, the potatoes that you have cut into cubes, the carrots, the onion that you have cut into thin strips.
6. In a bowl, make the vinaigrette with the vinegar, oil, salt and pepper.
7. Pour the vinaigrette into your salad bowl and stir, then adjust the seasoning.
8. Sprinkle with parsley.

A Cantonese in Reunion

Preparation : 1 hour   *Servings : 4 people*

INGREDIENTS

PREPARATION

- 500g basmati rice
- 200g smoked bacon
- 1 slice of 200 gr of ham (about 1/2cm once cut)
- 4 eggs
- 100g raw prawns
- 2 tablespoons of soy sauce
- 2 cloves garlic
- 1 bunch of chives (green onions)
- Salt (very little), pepper

1. Start by cooking the rice, it should not be sticky. I make it in the pressure cooker using the same amount of rice as water (3 glasses of rice = 3 glasses of water). Let the rice, oil and salt cool slightly and unmould a little with your fingers.
2. Rinse and finely chop the bunch of chives, it takes longer to do in the recipe and set aside.
3. Shell the raw prawns and cut them finely, marinate them in 2 tablespoons of soy sauce and a clove of garlic.
4. Cut the slice of ham into small cubes.
5. Beat the eggs into an omelette, add pepper and another clove of garlic. Cook the tortilla in a pan and cut it into small pieces or stir it. Remove from skillet and set aside.
6. Fry the bacon in the pan with a little oil. Remove and reserve. Do the same with the prawns.
7. Once the omelette, the prawns and the bacon are cooked, you can proceed to mixing.
8. In the saucepan over low heat, take half of the ingredients (ham, eggs, bacon, prawns and rice) mix well, repeat with the rest, so that everything is well mixed. Once all your ingredients are mixed, add the chopped chives and serve.

Boiled roast pork

Preparation : 15 mins   **Ready in: 08 min**   **Portions : 1 person**

INGREDIENTS

PREPARATION

- 1 roasted pork loin of about 1 kg
- 1 large onion coarsely chopped
- 4 carrots cut in 2
- 4 potatoes cut in 2
- 1 cabbage cut in large cartier, keeping the heart (so that it stands)
- Yellow beans to taste
- 4 tablespoons beef Bovril
- Salt pepper
- Butter

1. Put the butter in the pressure cooker (presto) and brown the roast on all sides, salt and pepper. Grilling it a lot is what will give it its flavour. Once the roast is golden brown, add the onion and brown it. After this step put water in the middle of the roast and add the Bovril. We start cooking quickly and when the pressure is at its maximum, we lower the heat to minimum (3-4) for about 2h30.
2. Meanwhile prepare the vegetables. When the meat is cooked, remove it from the presto and put the vegetables in the broth and cook for about 7-8 minutes. Serve hot.

Beef bourguignon- marengo

Preparation : 1 hour   Ready in : 50 min   Portions : 6 people

INGREDIENTS

- 500g beef
- 3 kg of carrots
- 1 case of mushrooms
- 1 onion
- 2 cloves garlic
- Flour
- 1/2 glass of cider vinegar
- 1 beef flavour cube
- 1 tablespoon of tomato puree
- Thyme/bay leaf
- olives
- 3 nails
- peppers

PREPARATION

1. Marinate the meat with the vinegar, 1/2 glass of water, cloves, pepper, thyme/bay leaf for three hours.
2. Brown the chopped onion and the crushed garlic in the olive oil; add the tomato purée then add the meat. Brown lightly before mixing with the flour. Put the marinade, the cube and add water to cover the meat, salt and cook for 30 minutes in the pressure cooker.
3. Cut the carrots into rounds.
4. Add the carrots, mushrooms and olives to the meat and continue cooking for another 20 minutes.

Rabbit with tarragon

Preparation : 15 mins   *Ready in : 1 hr 30 min*   *Servings : 4 people*

INGREDIENTS

PREPARATION

- 1 rabbit of 1.5 kg in pieces
- 30g butter
- 2 cases of olive oil
- A little flour
- 3 shallots
- 2 cloves garlic
- 4 sprigs of tarragon
- 1/3 bottle of white wine
- 250g mushrooms
- 100 g fresh cream
- Salt
- Pepper

1. Brown the pieces of rabbit on all sides (without reserving the liver) in a pan with 2 tablespoons of oil. As it browns, transfer the pieces to a saucepan. When all the pieces are in the pan, add 30 g of butter. Sprinkle with flour. Stir over high heat.

2. Mix the shallots and the minced garlic cloves, half the tarragon, the wine, 1 glass of water, salt and pepper. Cover and simmer for 1 hour in total (25 minutes in the pressure cooker). Clean and cut the mushrooms into strips. Add them to the pan halfway through cooking. Finely chop the remaining tarragon leaves in the cream, add 5 minutes before the end of cooking.

3. Serve after removing the bouquet garni and the tarragon stems.

Chicken breasts and fresh vegetables

Preparation : 45 mins   *Ready in: 25 min*   *Portions : 4 people*

INGREDIENTS

- 3 nice chicken breasts
- 400 g sand carrots
- 400g fresh mushrooms
- 250g potatoes
- 1 small green Espelette pepper
- 1 large shallot
- 150g grated ham
- 1 case of 125 g walnut cream cheese
- 40 cl of semi-thick cream 18°
- Espelette pepper
- Salt of Guarantee
- 1 chicken stock cube
- 20 to 25 cl of water
- 1 tablespoon cornstarch sauce

PREPARATION

1. Cut the carrots into sticks... The mushrooms into strips... The potatoes into cubes and the chopped shallot.
2. Heat 3 tablespoons of olive oil in your pressure cooker, add the shallot. Let brown gently... The carrots, then the mushrooms... Then the potatoes... and finally the chicken cube.
3. Let the mixture gently return for 6 to 8 minutes.
4. Add the grated ham... The cheese spread with walnuts and the lighter cream Pour 20 to 25 cl of water. Salt and pepper a little.
5. Lightly mix this preparation...
6. Place the chicken breasts on the vegetables... Sprinkle them with salt and Espelette pepper.
7. Pressurize for 13 minutes...
8. Remove the fillets, drizzle with the cornstarch sauce to thicken the sauce if necessary...

Asparagus with poached egg and black garlic

Preparation : 15 mins   **Ready in : 15 min**   **Portions : 1 person**

INGREDIENTS	PREPARATION

INGREDIENTS

- 5 nice asparagus
- 1 egg
- 1/2 teaspoon sesame oil
- 1 clove of black garlic (3/4 gr) (from Taste and health)
- Chive
- Gomasio
- Pepper

PREPARATION

1. Steam the asparagus (in a 12mm pressure cooker).
2. Cook the poached egg.
3. In a saucepan put 300 ml of water with 100 ml of white vinegar.
4. Put to boil.
5. Meanwhile, break the egg into a cup.
6. When the water boils, stir it with a fork and add the egg.
7. Bake 3mm.
8. Carefully remove the poached egg and pat it dry on paper towel.
9. Cut the black garlic into petals and chop the chives.
10. In a serving dish put the asparagus then the poached egg.
11. Drizzle with sesame oil, sprinkle with black garlic petals and chives.
12. Sprinkle lightly with Gomasio and pepper.
13. Server without waiting.

Rabbit, mushrooms, tomatoes

| Preparation : 15 mins | Ready in : 30 min | Portions : 4 people |

INGREDIENTS

- 1 rabbit of about 1.2 kg
- 2 chopped onions
- 1 knob of butter
- 1 case of old-fashioned mustard
- 1 good case of flour (or cornstarch)
- 1 small case of tomato purée
- 1 dose of gelatine chicken broth
- 1 glass of red wine
- 1 case of mushrooms
- 1 sprig of thyme
- Rosemary
- 1 sage leaf
- Salt
- Pepper

PREPARATION

1. Brown the rabbit pieces on all sides.
2. Season with salt, pepper.
3. Add chopped onions and sauté for 2-3 minutes.
4. Mix regularly.
5. Then add the mustard, the mushroom slices, 1 sprig of thyme, 1 sprig of rosemary, 1 sage leaf. To mix together.
6. Add the cornstarch, the stock cube, mix... Then the tomato puree, the wine and mix again.
7. Cook in the pressure cooker for 15-20 min.
8. After opening the pressure cooker, remove the sprigs of thyme, rosemary, sage leaf.

Pork with orange, and grand Marnier

Preparation : 15 mins   **Ready in: 30 min**   **Portions : 4 people**

INGREDIENTS

PREPARATION

- 1 kg pork loin
- 50cl of orange juice
- 3 untreated oranges
- 30g of butter
- 10 cl of orange liqueur (like Grand Marnier or Cointreau)
- 1 tablespoon cornstarch
- Salt
- Pepper

Wash the oranges, finely remove the zest, leaving the white skin on the fruit. Cut the zest into thin sticks and blanch it for 5 minutes in a small saucepan of boiling water. Drain, keeping the flavoured water.

Heat the butter in the pressure cooker and put the meat cut into pieces to brown on all sides. Then pour 50 cl of orange juice, salt and pepper, peel the oranges, removing all the white skin, cut them into slices and close the pressure cooker.

Increase the pressure to high heat, and as soon as the valve whispers, lower the heat and cook for 30 minutes.

In a bowl, mix 15 cl of water with the cornstarch. Turn off the heat under the pressure cooker, lower the pressure, then open the lid, remove the pieces of meat and pass the sauce through the grinder.

Return the pan to the heat and add the bowl with the cornstarch, mix well.

Turn off the heat under the pressure cooker, pour the zest and juice into the sauce, mix, reduce a little over high heat without covering.

Arrange the meat and oranges on a warm serving platter, cover with the zest sauce and serve immediately.

Cod couscous

Preparation : 15 mins   *Servings : 6 people*

INGREDIENTS

- 6 cod fillets
- 2 cases of tomato puree
- 3 tablespoons spicy couscous
- 1 teaspoon of harissa, raz elhanout, cumin
- 3 tomatoes
- 2 turnips
- 5 carrots
- 2 zucchinis
- 1 green and red bell pepper
- 1 box of chickpeas
- A lemon juices
- 1 lemon cut into wedges

PREPARATION

1. In a pressure cooker, pour 3 tablespoons of olive oil. Put the fire with a little spice and colour the fish when it is golden, add the vegetables, the tomato purée, the spicy couscous and the harissa with the juice and the pieces of lemon.
2. Cover with water, close the pressure cooker and cook for 25 minutes once the pressure has risen.
3. When the 25 minutes are up, release the steam from your pressure cooker, open and add the chickpeas.
4. Reheating: count 10 minutes of cooking once your pressure cooker is under pressure.
5. Serve with medium grains.

Veal with prunes (Moroccan tajine)

Preparation : 45 mins   *Servings : 4 people*

INGREDIENTS

- A handful of prunes
- Sesame seeds
- Roasted almonds
- Butter
- Olive oil
- Saffron
- Cinnamon ginger
- Honey

PREPARATION

1. Put the meat in your pressure cooker covered with water and leave to cook (observe)... During this time soak the prunes in water... Put them in a large saucepan add: the butter. Olive oil.

2. Saffron ginger. 2 tablespoons honey Cover with water and cook until melted and slightly caramelized. Meanwhile, your meat is cooked... Reduce the sauce to your liking, serve... Sprinkle your prunes with toasted sesame seeds

Kastu Curry - Curry rice *Japanese*

Preparation : 45 mins   **Ready in: 25 min**   **Portions : 2 people**

INGREDIENTS

- 150-200 g rice cooked in a pressure cooker,
- 2 fairly thin slices of pork (boneless loin),
- Panko (coarse Japanese breadcrumbs),
- 1 egg (for the breadcrumbs),
- Flour (for breadcrumbs),
- Frying oil,
- 2 large carrots,
- 3 medium potatoes,
- 1 large onion,
- Japanese curry (1 1/2 sachet of powder or 1 case of curry)
- 1200ml of water.

PREPARATION

1. Cut your onion, your carrots, your potatoes and brown them in a pan.
2. Once it sizzles nicely, add the water, then the curry and let brown for at least 25 minutes over medium-low heat (and stir often!).
3. The curry should form a thick sauce, so initially I recommend putting in just 1 liter and 3/4 of the curry and cooking for 20 minutes. Then, add the rest of the curry and the water and let everything come back for about 15 minutes over low heat.
4. All you have to do is take care of the meat. Cut it deep then:
5. Pass it in the flour, then in the beaten egg, then in the Panko. Then we put it to fry for a few minutes on one side then the other.
6. Drain the meat and cut it into strips 1/2 cm wide.
7. Place the rice on a large plate. Place your meat on it and finally pour your curry accompanied by the rice and a little on the meat.

Stew broth soup

Preparation : 15 mins   *Servings : 1 person*

INGREDIENTS	PREPARATION

- Pot au feu broth of the day
- Vermicelli

1. The stew was eaten at noon.
2. Meats and vegetables removed from the pressure cooker or pot allow the broth to freeze.
3. In the evening, at mealtimes, using a slotted spoon remove the frozen fat and.
4. Pass through a colander to filter the broth, at the bottom of the pan the remains.
5. Empty onto a plate.
6. Bring the broth to a boil and add the noodles to your liking thick or thin, leftovers are small pieces of vegetables celery, leeks, turnips, carrots and shredded meats add to the broth and serve immediately.

Roast pork and curls

Preparation : 15 mins   *Ready in _ : mins Servings : 4 people*

INGREDIENTS	PREPARATION

INGREDIENTS

- 1 roast pork tenderloin, about 2 kg
- 2 spoons of butter
- Salt pepper
- 1 large onion, quartered
- 4-5 tablespoons beef Bovril soup
- Hot water halfway through cooking

PREPARATION

1. Brown the butter and put the roast. Salt and pepper. Brown the roast on all sides so that it is dark, this is what will give the right flavour to your broth. Then add the onion to brown it. At the end of this step add the Bovril and hot water. When the pressure is at maximum, lower the heat to low for about 2½ to 3 hours, depending on the size of the roast.

Buckles:

2. Remove the pork roast, add hot water, Bovril to the meat just to get a dark broth. Bring to a boil and add the curls, mix well and cook to your liking. Serve hot with the roast. A true delight.

Lamb shoulder with carrots and dates

Preparation : 1 hour   **Ready in : 30 min**   **Portions : 6 people**

INGREDIENTS

PREPARATION

- 1 kg lamb shoulder, cut into pieces
- 2 onions
- 1 small bunch of parsley and coriander
- 1 tomato, diced
- 1 crushed garlic clove
- 1 cinnamon stick
- 2 cases of olive oil
- 1 teaspoon of salt
- 1 case of four spice mix
- 1 teaspoon paprika
- 1/2 teaspoon ras el hanout
- 1/2 teaspoon ground cinnamon
- 500g carrots
- 200g pitted dates
- 50g of honey
- 50g of butter
- 1/2 teaspoon ground cinnamon

1. In a pot, brown your meat with olive oil, add the onions, brown, mix well and scrape their juices from the bottom of the pot. Add a large glass of water, your spices, the crushed garlic clove, the parsley and the coriander. Cook for half an hour and add your diced tomatoes. Continue cooking, the meat should be tender and melted. You can use a pressure cooker, but be careful not to drown the meat, you will lose all the flavours. When the meat is cooked, remove it from the pan and keep it warm.

2. Peel and wash the carrots, cut them into slices half a centimetre wide. Cook or steam, or in salted water. When they are cooked, drain them and set aside.

3. In the pot, pour your pitted dates with sugar, butter and cinnamon, add water if necessary. Leave to cook over low heat until a syrupy and melting sauce is obtained, at this stage add the carrots, cook over low heat for five minutes, then the pieces of shoulder, keep on the heat for another five minutes.

4. Serve hot with good homemade bread.

Creole au gratin cork bread

Preparation : 15 mins   **Ready in : 20 mins**   **Portions : 1 person**

INGREDIENTS

- Bread
- Plugs
- Grated cheese
- Mayonnaise or ketchup or chili
- Fries (optional)

PREPARATION

1. Cook your corks: Freeze your corks in the pressure cooker basket and cook for about 20 minutes from the moment the water boils. To check for doneness, stick a knife in and if it goes through, they're done.

2. Cut a piece of bread, open it lengthwise, add your sauce (at the session we like to put the three ketchup, mayonnaise and chilli). Top with grated cheese and bake until cheese melts.

3. You can also add some fries before the grated cheese, it's even better.

Pumpkin-sweet potato-coconut milk soup

Preparation : 15 mins   *Servings : 6 people*

INGREDIENTS

- 3 carrots
- A pumpkin
- 2 sweet potatoes
- 250ml coconut milk
- Curry to taste (for me 1/2cc)
- Salt
- Pepper

PREPARATION

1. Peel and cut the vegetables into pieces, put them in the pressure cooker with water, salt and pepper.
2. When the vegetables are cooked, mix them in your blinder with the coconut milk, the curry and add the cooking broth according to the thickness you want for your soup. Add salt and pepper if necessary.

Veal tongue with caper sauce

Preparation : 1 hour 30 minutes   *Ready in: 50 min*   *Portions : 4 people*

INGREDIENTS

- 1 veal tongue
- 2 tablespoons of capers
- 1 chopped onion
- 3 pickles
- 3 shallots, chopped
- 20 cl of liquid cream
- 20g butter
- 1 egg yolk
- 1 tablespoon of flour
- Salt pepper

PREPARATION

1. Blanch the tongue in salted water with a little vinegar, 10 min in the pressure cooker.
2. Remove the skin from the tongue.
3. In a saucepan, brown the onions and shallots in the butter. Sprinkle with flour.
4. Gradually add 2 glasses of water. Salt pepper. Add capers and sliced pickles.
5. Cut the tongue into slices, put it in the sauce for 30 minutes over low heat.
6. In a bowl, dissolve the egg yolk in the liquid cream.
7. Remove the tongue slices from the pan.
8. Turn off the heat and slowly pour the egg cream into the sauce, whisking.
9. Serve hot.

Homemade rabbit pâté

Preparation : 3 h   **Ready in : 2 hrs**   **Servings : 6 people**

INGREDIENTS

- 1 rabbit of 1.5 kg
- 1/4 the rabbit's weight in pork
- 1/4 the rabbit's weight in lard
- 1 carrot
- 2 onions
- 1 bunch of herbs
- Garlic
- 5 cl cognac
- 10 g of salt per kilo
- 3g pepper
- 1 egg

PREPARATION

1. Bone the rabbit, make a jus with the bones by browning them in the fat with 1 carrot and 1 chopped onion. Add 1 liter of cold water, the bouquet garni and the garlic, cook for 1 hour. Strain and reduce the juice to have 20 cl.
2. Chop the meat with 1 onion, add 5 cl of cognac, 20 cl of juice, 10 g of salt, 3 g of pepper, 1 egg.
3. Cook in a terrine filled with fatty or smoked bacon for 1 hour at 180°.
   Where
4. In terrines or small jars with 1 bay leaf in each pâté and sterilize for 3 hours at 100° in a pressure cooker.
5. It is possible to replace pork and pork fat with sausage meat (same weight as rabbit meat).
6. It is possible to replace the bone juice with reduced chicken broth.

Beef dauphine potatoes

Preparation : 15 mins   Ready in : 4 hrs   Servings : 1 person

INGREDIENTS

- 1 roast beef stew
- Carrots
- Mushrooms
- Shallots
- Dauphine potatoes

PREPARATION

1. Put a little oil and butter in the pressure cooker, add the mushrooms and carrots and brown them. To book.
2. Add a little butter and brown the roast with the shallots on all sides, when the juice browns, add about 1 glass of water, close the pan and cook over low heat for 1/2 hour.
3. Cut the roast into thin slices (normally it should lack juice so deglaze and add water).
4. Return to the pan and cook for another 1/2 hour (depending on the meat).
5. At the end add the mushrooms, carrots.

Golden ball beetroot, red beetroot and raspberries

Preparation : 15 mins   Ready in : 2 hrs 30 mins   Portions : 4 people

INGREDIENTS

- Rice cakes
- 1 cooked red beet
- As many raspberries as red beets
- 1 golden ball beet
- Ricotta
- Salt pepper
- Raspberry or fig vinegar

PREPARATION

1. Cook your golden ball beets to your liking. (Steam, pressure cooker, oven, I chose the melting result for 2h30 in simmering water.
2. Meanwhile, mix the beets with the raspberries, salt, pepper and a dash of raspberry vinegar.
3. Put this preparation in a piping bag. Book cool
4. Also put your ricotta in a piping bag.
5. When the golden ball beets are cooked, using an apple corer, remove the tubes or, failing that, the balls with a mini abacus.
6. Book cool
7. 1 hour before serving, place on a rice cake and sprinkle with fresh herbs.

Indian chicken parmentier

Preparation : 30 mins   **Ready in : 40 min**   **Portions : 4 people**

INGREDIENTS

PREPARATION

- 600g potato
- 10 cl of milk
- 50g butter
- 4 chicken cutlets (diced)
- 1 onion
- 1 tablespoon vegetable oil
- 1 tablespoon olive oil
- 1/2 lemon
- 10 cl heavy cream
- 10 cl coconut cream
- 1 tablespoon of curry
- 30g toasted slivered almonds
- 2 tablespoons fine breadcrumbs
- Nutmeg
- Salt
- Ground pepper

1. Peel potatoes. Steam them or cook them in a pressure cooker. Run them through the vegetable mill. Add the very hot milk, 30 g of butter in pieces, nutmeg, pepper, salt.
2. Mix this puree well, it must be quite firm. Finely chop the onion, brown it and caramelize it in the oil, in a pan, for a few minutes. In another skillet, sauté and brown the diced chicken in the olive oil for a few minutes.
3. Sprinkle with curry. Pour in the heavy cream and coconut cream. Let this chicken curry reduce a bit. Add the juice of half a lemon. Preheat the oven to 200°C (Th. 6-7). Divide the chicken curry between the pans. Add the caramelized onion and slivered almonds.
4. Let cool. Fill with puree and smooth with a spatula. Sprinkle lightly with breadcrumbs, add a little butter. Bake and roast in the oven for 15 to 20 minutes.

Milanese Osso Bucco

INGREDIENTS	PREPARATION

INGREDIENTS

- 1Kg 500 to 1Kg 800 sliced veal shank
- Cad slice with bone
- 3 fresh tomatoes, i.e., 600 g
- 1 clove of garlic
- 1 onion
- 1 bunch of herbs
- 2 cm lemon zest
- + Zest on sticks
- 1 tablespoon of tomato puree
- 1 tablespoon oil
- A little flour
- 80g of butter
- 1 glass of dry white wine
- 1 glass of water
- Grated parmesan or gruyere cheese
- Salt pepper
- 300g of rice
- 1 glass of cognac liqueur

PREPARATION

1. Dredge the pieces of meat in the flour, brown them well in the pressure cooker with the butter and oil over high heat (for a creamy sauce, drizzle with cognac and flambé).
2. Then add the chopped onion, the white wine, the water, the tablespoon of concentrate, the bouquet garni and the peeled and crushed garlic, salt and pepper.
3. Close the pressure cooker and simmer for 25 minutes from the pressure setting.
4. Meanwhile, pour the rice into the wire basket; plunge everything into a large saucepan with cold salted water and bring to a boil for 10 minutes, remove the basket from the saucepan and drain the rice in it.
5. 10 minutes before the end of cooking the ossobuco, open the pressure cooker, remove the bouquet garni and add the peeled, seeded and diced tomatoes, the piece of lemon zest, cover with the basket of rice and close the lid. pressure cooker to finish cooking about 10 minutes.
6. To serve, shell the rice in a deep plate, pour the ossobuco and the sauce in the centre, sprinkle with sticks of lemon zest and present a little grated cheese on the side.

Mom Cathy's Chicken Rice

Preparation : 30 mins　　　*Ready in : 20 mins*　　　*Portions : 4 people*

INGREDIENTS

- 1 meaty hen
- 1 liter of dry white wine
- 2 carrots
- 1 piece of celery
- 1 leek
- 2 onions
- 3 cloves _
- 2 cloves garlic
- 1 bunch of herbs
- Salt and pepper
- 25 cl heavy cream
- 50g of butter
- 50g flour
- 2 glasses of rice (1/2 glass per person, glass of mustard)

PREPARATION

1. Put the chicken in a pressure cooker and drizzle it with white wine. Add the carrots cut into rings, the chopped leek, the chopped celeriac, 1 whole onion sprinkled with cloves, the garlic and the bouquet garbni.
2. Add water to the height of the hen. Close the pressure cooker and cook for 45 minutes. At the end of cooking, remove the chicken and place it on a plate. Strain the cooking juices and set aside.
3. In a frying pan, melt 25 g of butter. As soon as it melts, pour in the flour, stirring briskly to avoid lumps. Gradually pour in the cooking juices from the chicken to obtain a smooth sauce. Adjust the seasoning.
4. Add the fresh cream and the chicken that you have cut into pieces. Bring to a boil.
5. Meanwhile, melt 25g of butter in an ovenproof saucepan. Heat this tea. 9. Add a chopped onion and sauté gently. When the onion is well coloured, add the thyme, stir.
6. Add the rice and stir. The rice should take on a nice colour. Add the cooking juice (2x 1/2 volume of rice). Bring to the boil and cook for 20 minutes at 180°C. 6, not a minute more.

Plain spare ribs, bacon, Potatoes and Brussels sprouts

| Preparation : 30 mins | Ready in : 30 min | Portions : 2 people |

INGREDIENTS

- 500 g plain spare ribs
- 2 slices of smoked bacon
- Salt
- Pepper
- 500 g Brussels sprouts
- 1mg hazelnut
- 4-5 potatoes

PREPARATION

1. Cut into portions of 4-5 bones, depending on size.
2. Salt and pepper.
3. Brown the ribs and bacon in the pressure cooker with a little fat.
4. When they have taken colour, add a little water and continue cooking in the pressure cooker for 30 minutes over very low heat when the pressure cooker has risen.
5. When the meat is cooked, set aside.
6. Deglaze with 10-20 cl of water.
7. Add clean Brussels sprouts and potatoes... In salted water.
8. Cook under pressure for 8 to 10 minutes.
9. Eat it all hot.

Quick Veal Osso Bucco

Preparation : 15 mins   **Ready in : 20 mins**   **Portions : 2 people**

INGREDIENTS

- 1 onion
- 1 clove of garlic
- 1/2-1 carrot
- 1 stalk of celery
- Salt pepper
- 1 case of flour
- 1 case of olive oil
- 1 knob of butter
- 1 pinch of powdered beef stock
- 200ml strained tomatoes
- 1 bunch of herbs
- 10-15 Dl of dry white wine
- 1 pinch of powdered beef stock
- 2 slices of veal osso Bucco

PREPARATION

1. Chop the onion and the germ-free garlic clove if necessary.
2. Cut the clean carrot into small dice.
3. Finely chop the small stalk of celery,
4. Reserve the twigs for garnish.
5. Season the osso Bucco slices with salt and pepper.
6. Pass them in the flour, hit them to remove the excess flour.
7. Pour 1 case of olive oil and the butter into the pressure cooker.
8. Brown the osso Bucco slices.
9. Remove and reserve the meat.
10. Brown the onion, the minced garlic clove, the carrot and the celery over low heat for 5 minutes, stirring.
11. Add the white wine and 1 pinch of powdered veal stock.
12. To put out the fire.
13. Pour the tomatoes.
14. Add the bouquet garni.
15. Return the meat to the pan.
16. Close the pressure cooker and cook for 12 minutes as gently as possible after putting it under pressure.
17. Adjust seasoning.
18. Serve with fresh pasta.

Lamb with tomatoes

Preparation : 50 mins   *Servings : 4 people*

INGREDIENTS	PREPARATION

INGREDIENTS

- 1 onion
- 1 carrot
- 1 knob of butter
- 1 case of flour
- 600g neck (or neck) of lamb
- 2 cases of oil
- 1 case of tomato coulis
- 1 clove of garlic
- Sprig of aromatic herbs
- 1 pinch of cumin seeds
- 2-3 sprigs of fresh thyme
- 20 cl of red wine (or water)
- Salt
- Pepper
- Parsley

PREPARATION

1. Fry the onion and carrot slices in a knob of butter.
2. Brown the pieces of lamb on all sides in the hot oil.
3. Sprinkle them with flour.
4. Add onions and carrots.
5. To mix together.
6. Moisten with wine/water.
7. Mix again.
8. Add the tomato pulp, the bouquet garni,
9. Aromatic herbs, crushed garlic clove, salt, pepper.
10. Close the pressure cooker
11. Turn the pressure cooker on high.
12. As soon as the valve whispers, lower the heat.
13. Leave to cook for around 20 mins. on slow fire.
14. Adjust the seasoning if necessary.
15. Pour the pieces on a hot plate,
16. Topped with the cooking sauce,
17. Sprinkled with flat-leaf parsley.

Curly green cabbage with Liégeoise sauce

Preparation : 30 mins

Ready in _ : 2 hrs 30 mins Portions : 2 people

INGREDIENTS

- 1 kale
- Pork ribs
- 4 potatoes
- 2 fresh sausages (pork and beef), optional
- Salt pepper
- 2 cloves garlic
- + thyme, bay leaf (to taste)

PREPARATION

1. Wash the cabbage, drain it, cut it into strips.
2. Blanch it, 5-10 min, in salted boiling water.
3. When it is cooked, drain it, squeeze it.
4. .... Already prepared in the freezer!
5. Separately, in a large pot (all the "hotpot" should go in), brown the ribs.
6. Salt, pepper (add thyme, bay leaf to taste).
7. Add 2 peeled and chopped garlic cloves.
8. Cover with hot water to the top.
9. After boiling, lower the heat and simmer for about 1 hour. (Or in the pressure cooker for 20 min).
10. Then place the cabbage and diced potatoes on top,
11. As well as the fried sausages, about 3/4 h (10 min in the pressure cooker).
12. To mix together.
13. Reseason if necessary.
14. Serve.
15. Serve with pickles and mustard.

Dijon style lentils

Preparation : 15 mins   **Ready in: 5 to 10 min**   **Servings : 3 people**

INGREDIENTS

- 500g lentils
- 10 Knacks
- 3 beef stock cubes
- 100 g of bacon
- 4 slices of ham
- 3 cases of mustard
- 3 cases of liquid cream
- Butter
- Salt and pepper
- 5 Cloves _
- 1 onion
- 1 tablespoon of flour

PREPARATION

1. Put 3 litters of water in a pressure cooker. Add 3 beef stock cubes, the lentils. Plant the cloves in the onion and add it. Cook 10 minutes after whistling, no more.
2. Cut the hams into cubes and reserve them on a plate with the whole knacks.
3. When the lentils are cooked, let them drain, remove the onion and reserve the cooking juices.
4. Fry the bacon in the butter over low heat and let them brown, then add 1 case of flour.
5. Then add 5 good ladles of cooking juice, add 3 compartments of mustard and 3 compartments of cream. Salt pepper. Add the lentils, ham and knacks.

Savoyard tomatoes

Preparation : 30 mins   Servings : 2 people

INGREDIENTS	PREPARATION

INGREDIENTS

- 2 potatoes
- 1/2 onion
- 2 large tomatoes
- 1 tablespoon chopped parsley
- 60 g of reblochon
- Nutmeg
- Salt
- Pepper

PREPARATION

1. Cook the potatoes in boiling water or in a pressure cooker.
2. Remove the seeds and hollow out the tomatoes, then sprinkle the inside lightly.
3. Brown the onions in a non-stick skillet.
4. Add the peeled potatoes, chopped parsley, nutmeg, salt and pepper and mix.
5. Stuff each tomato with this preparation and cover with 1 small slice of Reblochon.
6. Grill the stuffed tomatoes for 10 to 15 minutes on the grill at 250°C.

Gratin of Christophanies from Martin Caribe

| Preparation : 1 hour | Ready in : 55 min | Portions : 4 people |

INGREDIENTS

PREPARATION

- 2/3 Christina
- 2 slices of smoked ham
- 1 onion
- 4 spring onions
- 1 clove of garlic
- Parsley
- Thyme
- butter oil
- Béchamel cheese breadcrumbs grater

1. Cut the Christos in 2... Remove the core and cook them in salted boiling water (30/40 min) or to go faster (pressure cooker). Remove the meat with a spoon, keeping the skin intact. Mix this meat. Brown the ham, onion, finely chopped chives and parsley, brown in a little oil. Mix with mashed potatoes and bechamel sauce. Stuff the Christophanies put breadcrumbs and Gruyere a few knots of hazelnut butter 10/15 min.

2. For the béchamel, prepare it or buy it already prepared.

3. Serve very hot.

Veal stew

Preparation : 15 mins   Ready in : 1 hr 30 min   Servings : 2 people

INGREDIENTS	PREPARATION

INGREDIENTS

- 250 G of veal in the collar for connoisseurs
- 20g butter
- 1 full tablespoon of flour
- 1 onion
- 1 beef broth
- 1 carrot
- 1 bunch of herbs
- Salt
- Pepper
- Chopped parsley
- 2 Cloves _

PREPARATION

1. Brown the meat lightly in a pan with 20 g of butter, the carrot and the chopped onion. Sprinkle the whole tablespoon with flour. Mix to let them cook a little, add the parsley, salt and pepper.

2. Add the broth previously prepared, the bouquet garni, 2 cloves, salt, pepper. Blanket. Leave to simmer for about 1h15 (25 minutes in the pressure cooker).

Monkfish with spicy West Indian sauce

Preparation : 15 mins   **Ready in : 15 min**   **Portions : 3 people**

INGREDIENTS

- 500g frozen skinless monkfish
- 250 g frozen large peeled prawns
- 350 g West Indian sauce
- 100 g frozen pepper strips in 3 colours
- 200g of rice
- 20 cl of semi - thick cream
- 100ml water

PREPARATION

1. Heat a tablespoon of olive oil with a knob of butter in your pressure cooker.
2. Add the frozen pepper strips, the pieces of monkfish and the frozen prawns that you have previously rinsed in cold water and cook over low heat for 3 minutes
3. Pour the rice Add the semi thick cream and the spicy tomato sauce then the water Mix everything
4. Cook 7 minutes from boiling

Green lentils with smoked pork blade & Toulouse sausages

Preparation : 15 mins   **Ready in: 1 hr 30 min**   **Servings : 4 people**

INGREDIENTS

- 1 smoked pork shoulder with bone of 780 gr
- 4 Toulouse pork sausages
- 6 small sand carrots
- 1 small case of cherry tomatoes
- 1 serving of about 5 tablespoons frozen homemade African tomato sauce
- 1 gold maggi cube
- 1 vegetable stock cube
- 1 bunch of herbs
- 3 medium onions
- 2 heads of garlic
- 2 cloves _
- 4 medium potatoes
- 3 tablespoons of olive oil

PREPARATION

1. Cook the shoulder for 45 minutes in the cold water of your pressure cooker, a chopped onion with 2 cloves, a vegetable stock cube and pepper.
2. Once the blade is cooked, we remove it and remove the broth that will not serve me.
3. In the pot, pour a drizzle of olive oil, lightly sauté the chopped onion and garlic Then the sausages put back the shoulder add the carrots cut into quarters The tomatoes and the African Pepper sauce Pour a glass of water and simmer for about 5 minutes Add the lentils, the potatoes cut in 2 or whole and cover with cold water. Don't forget the bouquet garni and the maggi golden cube.
4. Cook the meat and vegetables again for 25 minutes.
5. Dress and serve immediately

Cauliflower parmentier

Preparation : 15 mins   *Servings : 4 people*

INGREDIENTS	PREPARATION

- 400g ground beef
- 6 large potatoes
- 1 onion
- 1 cauliflower
- Liquid cream (about 10 cl)
- 1 beef stock cube
- Salt, pepper, oil, nutmeg
- Grated cheese to taste

1. Cook the cauliflower cut into florets with the peeled potatoes and wash in the pressure cooker for about 10-15 minutes.
2. Meanwhile, brown the chopped onion in a little oil, add the minced meat. Add the beef bouillon cube with a glass of water and cook until evaporated.
3. When the potatoes and the cauliflower are cooked, mix them with the cream, salt, pear and add the nutmeg before mixing. Also season the meat, place it in the bottom of a gratin dish, add the mashed potatoes and cauliflower and sprinkle with grated cheese put in the oven. 6 for about 15 minutes

Hummus, chickpea cream

Preparation : 15 mins   **Ready in : 2 hrs**   **Servings : 6 people**

INGREDIENTS

- 1 case 4/4 chickpeas
- 2 lemons
- 4 tablespoons of flour
- 2 cloves garlic
- 1/2 teaspoon cumin
- Salt,
- Olive oil
- Cumin, sweet pepper for seasoning

PREPARATION

1. In the jar of a blender, put all the ingredients: drained chickpeas (reserve 1 tablespoon of whole chickpeas for the last portion), flour (shake the jar well before use), cumin, garlic, lemon juice (start by adding the juice of one and a half lemons) and salt and mix from time to time. For another (beater stopped) by unsticking some of the ingredients that stick to the walls of the blender, add a little water if necessary. You need a fairly thick and creamy sauce, with the consistency of mayonnaise. Taste and adjust the seasoning if necessary (lemon juice or salt). Arrange in molds, sprinkle with paprika and cumin, pile a little hummus or a sprig of parsley in the centre to decorate and drizzle with olive oil.

Vegetable soup

Preparation : 15 mins *Servings : 8 people*

INGREDIENTS

- 50g butter
- 4 to 5 potatoes
- 2 onions
- 5 tomatoes
- 4 zucchinis
- 3 nice carrots
- Green salad
- Parsley
- Salt and pepper and 3 litters of water.
- All other vegetables are fine.

PREPARATION

1. Wash and prepare all your vegetables, cut them into pieces. Melt the butter in your pressure cooker, add all the vegetables, salt and pepper, add 3 litters of water and close your pan. When the valve whispers count 30 min. Kitchen.
2. Mix your soup and serve in bowls, sprinkle with parsley.

Moroccan mhamer (oven-grilled lamb chops)

Preparation : 45 mins   **Ready in : 30 min**   **Portions : 4 people**

INGREDIENTS

- 1 onion
- 4 garlic cloves
- Salt
- Pepper
- peppers
- Turmeric
- Ginger
- Olive oil
- 2 bars of olive oil

PREPARATION

1. This recipe is prepared in three steps: **First time** Take it all
2. Ingredients Marinate the meat the night before. **Step 2:** Take your
3. Pressure cooker cover everything with water and cook for 30 minutes.
4. Open and check that it is ready. The meat should be very tender. To enlarge.
5. Cooking time if necessary. **3rd time** During cooking, reduce the.
6. Sauce while you have already put the meat in the oven.
7. Dress your dish with a little sauce first then on the meat.
8. Serve with fries or sautéed vegetables with voucher.
9. Glass of mint tea

Moroccan Cardoon Tagine

Preparation : 15 mins   **Ready in : 20 mins**   **Portions : 4 people**

INGREDIENTS

- 4 Noble piece of veal
- 4 garlic cloves
- 2 tablespoons of natural oil
- 3 tablespoons of olive oil
- Salt
- Pepper
- Ginger
- Turmeric
- Mild red pepper
- A pile of pre-washed thistles
- A handful of red olives. A candied lemon

PREPARATION

1. Take a pressure cooker place your meat in the middle and put on it all the ingredients mentioned with the spices Cover with water close your pressure cooker Cook for 20 minutes Open mix the thistles close until the meat is completely cooked put your olives and candied lemon Let simmer over low heat Let the sauce reduce to your liking, but not too much Taste

Rfissa (traditional dish from greater Casablanca and surroundings)

Preparation : 15 mins   *Servings : 4 people*

INGREDIENTS	PREPARATION

For the sauce:

- Provide 4 good pieces of chicken per person.
- 120 grams of green lentils.
- 2 large onions cut into small pieces (not grated)
- A bunch of herbs.
- Stale butter.
- Pepper
- Ginger
- Turmeric.
- U, good hint of special pieces for this dish, say "msakhen" or default raz el hanout
- Half an egg per person + a handful of raisins (optional... It's not originally in this dish but it's great with don't deprive yourself of it, you have to cook them alone and not with the sauce))

1. For the sauce: put everything in your pressure cooker... Brown well... Cover with water... Leave to cook... Leave the sauce to taste.
2. For the Rfissa leaf... Either it's super fine homemade .... Or ... Bring good quality semen ... Cut into pieces according to the quantity requested ... Steam ... Then prepare your plate to eat "hot ... But it's a good...

Fricassee of zucchini - potatoes with curry and mint

Preparation : 15 mins   *Servings : 3 people*

INGREDIENTS	PREPARATION

INGREDIENTS

- 3 organic courgettes
- 3 potatoes
- 1 sweet red onion
- 2 cloves garlic
- 1 fresh tomato
- 1 sprig of fresh thyme
- 3 sprigs of fresh mint
- 1 tablespoon of olive and rapeseed oil
- 1 tbsp curry powder
- Salt pepper

PREPARATION

1. Peel and cut the potatoes in half, pre-cook them in the MO or pressure cooker.
2. Cut the ends of the courgettes, if they are organic, do not peel them, cut them into cubes.
3. In a saucepan, pour the olive oil and the rapeseed, lightly colour the peeled and chopped sweet onion, add the zucchini, thyme, mint, peeled and crushed garlic, salt and lightly pepper; leave to brown for one to two minutes without burning, add the pruned tomato, the curry and the pre-cooked and chopped potatoes, add ¼ to ½ liter of water;
4. Bring to the boil to finish cooking the potatoes, which should be tender.
5. You don't need more juice but don't let it stick either, remove the sprig of thyme.
6. Serve with beef, roast, turkey, chicken, pork.

Coconut chicken

Preparation : 15 mins   *Ready in : 20 mins*   *Portions : 4 people*

INGREDIENTS

- 1 large onion
- 4 pieces of chicken
- 20 cl of coconut milk
- 100g grated coconut
- 1 tablespoon crushed peanuts
- Tomato
- Salt
- Pepper
- Olive oil

PREPARATION

1. Fry the chicken pieces in the oil and set aside.
2. Cut and slice the onion and cook over low heat, then add the chicken pieces.
3. Mix the tomato (1 teaspoon) in a glass of water and pour it over the chicken. Add coconut milk, grated coconut and crushed peanuts. Withdraw.
4. Close the pressure cooker and cook for 20 minutes.
5. You can accompany this dish with rice.

Large white Spanish beans in tomato sauce with Provençal herbs

---

Preparation : 30 mins   **Ready in: 25 min**   **Portions : 6 people**

INGREDIENTS

- 500g large white beans
- 1 small case of tomato coulis
- 2 onions
- 2 cloves garlic
- Herbs of Provence

PREPARATION

1. Brown the chopped onions in a little olive oil. When they are lightly coloured, add the crushed garlic, tomato coulis and Provence herbs. Season. Simmer this sauce base over low heat for 5 minutes, then add the beans and 500ml of water.
2. Cook in the pressure cooker for 20 min.
3. Note: for a better taste, the ideal is to use fresh beans, but otherwise, soak the dried beans the day before preparation.

Tongue with cold meat sauce

Preparation : 15 mins   **Ready in : 1 hr 55 min**   **Servings : 6 people**

INGREDIENTS

- A beef tongues
- 1 onion
- 1 tooth
- Salt pepper
- 1 bay leaf
- 1 leek
- 2 carrots

For the sauce:

- 30g of butter
- 30g flour
- 1 shallot
- 2dl of white wine
- Tongue Broth 3dl
- 50g pickle
- 1 teaspoon of mustard
- Salt pepper

PREPARATION

1. Blanch your tongue then cooks it in a pressure cooker with all the ingredients for at least 1h30. Remove the skin and cut into slices, keep warm. Add sliced pickles.

Preparing the charcuterie sauce:

2. Put the butter and the shallot in a sauce boat, brown, add the flour, cook for a few minutes then add the liquids (white wine and broth) but not all at once to adjust the consistency of the sauce. Cook for about 20 minutes then add the mustard. Adjust the seasoning if necessary.

3. Strain the sauce and pour it over the tongue.

4. Serve with white rice.

Chicken with olives and potatoes

Preparation : 30 mins　　　**Ready in : 1 h 03 min**　　　**Servings : 4 people**

INGREDIENTS

PREPARATION

- 4 chicken thighs
- 300g pitted green olives
- 5 large potatoes
- 1 tomato
- 1 large chopped onion
- 4 garlic cloves, minced
- 10 cl or 5 tablespoons of olive oil
- 1/2 bunch cilantro, chopped
- 1 teaspoon of ginger
- 1 teaspoon paprika
- 1 teaspoon of turmeric
- A pinch of chilli
- A pinch of saffron
- 1/2 lemon (untreated) cut into small cubes
- Juice of 1/2 lemon
- 1 liter and a half of water
- Salt and pepper

1. Prepare a "chermoula" or marinade with the onion, garlic, coriander, juice of half a lemon, olive oil, all the spices, salt and pepper.
2. Marinate the chicken thighs in this "chermoula".
3. Let the thighs marinate for as long as possible.
4. Put the chicken thighs in a pressure cooker or pressure cooker and brown them lightly.
5. As soon as they are golden brown, add all the marinade and add the tomato cut into small cubes as well as the half lemon cut into small cubes.
6. Brown for 3 minutes uncovered and add the equivalent of a liter and a half of water. Close the pan and cook for about twenty minutes (as soon as the pan begins to whistle).
7. Remove the chicken thighs and put them in the oven until golden brown with crispy skin (about 15 to 20 minutes in a preheated oven at 180°).
8. Desalinate the olives by plunging them into boiling water for a good 5 minutes and rinsing them well.
9. In the pan where the chicken was cooked, put the potatoes cut into very thick cubes and the previously rinsed and desalted olives. Close the pan and cook for another twenty minutes.

Shepherd's pie potato, celeriac, carrots

Preparation : 30 mins   **Ready in : 40 min**   **Portions : 8 people**

INGREDIENTS

PREPARATION

- 6 large potatoes
- 500gr of fresh steak, chopped (for me from the butcher)
- 1 celeriac
- 4 carrots
- 1 or 2 shallots
- Salt pepper
- Butter
- 1 packet of Gruyere cheese

1. Peel the potatoes and the carrots and the celeriac, cut the potatoes in 4 and the celery in pieces and 2 carrots in slices and the other 2 carrots in very small pieces, wash all the vegetables put the potatoes in the pressure cooker 2 carrots and celeriac is filled with salted water and cooked 20/30 minutes after the whistle, in a small saucepan with water the carrot pieces are also cooked. Once the vegetables are cooked, puree the vegetable grinders in a vegetable grinder in a bowl with salt and put a good chunk of butter to mix. In a baking dish, sprinkle with a few pieces of butter and pour half of the mashed potatoes and set aside meanwhile in a saucepan put a small piece of butter to melt and add the shallots, thinly sliced until they are golden, add the small pieces of carrots and cook for a few minutes and add the ground beef slightly salted and peppered and cook for a few minutes, once cooked spread the puree everywhere and cover with the rest of the puree well spread and sprinkle with grated Gruyere bake in a hot oven at 180/200 degrees for about 40 minutes until the Gruyere is golden brown.
2. It's delicious with a green salad.

Endive gratin with parmesan sauce

Preparation : 30 mins   **Ready in : 30 min**   **Portions : 4 people**

INGREDIENTS

- 1 kg endive
- Milk
- Cornstarch
- Salt
- Pepper
- Nutmeg
- Parmesan cheese
- Smoked ham matchsticks

PREPARATION

1. Start by cleaning the endives, cook them for 20 minutes in the pressure cooker, once cooked, drain them.
2. Meanwhile prepare the sauce, heat the milk, bring to the boil then pour the cornstarch to thicken, add salt, pepper, nutmeg then the parmesan, to this preparation add the smoked ham matches, mix.
3. Take a gratin dish, butter the bottom of the dish, put the cooked endives, then pour the sauce, cook for 30 minutes, th: 200.

Mashed potatoes, parsnip & chicory/endive

Preparation : 15 mins   **Ready in : 30 min**   **Portions : 2 people**

INGREDIENTS

- 2 potatoes
- 2 parsnip roots
- 1 chicory / escarole
- 15cl of milk
- 1 egg yolk
- 1 knob of butter
- Salt pepper
- Peanut
- Fresh cream (optional)

PREPARATION

1. Peel the potatoes and parsnips.
2. Clean and cut the chicory/escarole into strips.
3. Cook everything in salted water for about 20-30 minutes (10 minutes in a pressure cooker).
4. Shred everything... Depending on taste, large pieces... Mousseline.
5. Add egg yolk, butternut squash, milk, salt, pepper and nutmeg.
6. Possibly fresh cream if you want a creamier purée.
7. Mix everything.
8. Add milk if the dough is not soft enough.
9. Fresh herbs (parsley, chives, etc.) if desired.
10. Gratinate with a little cheese.

Squash gratin with flora line

Preparation : 15 mins   **Ready in : 20 mins**   **Portions : 4 people**

INGREDIENTS

- 500g pumpkin
- 1/2 liter of milk
- Flora line
- 100g grated cheese
- Salt, pepper, garlic powder

PREPARATION

1. Steam the pumpkin for 10 minutes in a pressure cooker and mash it in the bottom of a gratin dish, sprinkle with salt, pepper and garlic powder.
2. Preheat your oven to 200°C.
3. Boil the milk in a saucepan and pour in the flora line, salt and pepper.
4. Pour over the pumpkin and sprinkle with grated cheese.
5. Cook for 15 minutes at 200°C.

Purslane, beetroot and feta salad, orange vinaigrette sauce

Preparation : 15 mins   Ready in : 5 to 10 min   Servings : 2 people

INGREDIENTS

- 200g purslane
- 1 small cooked beet (2-3 very small)
- 1 shallot
- 50g feta
- 2 boiled eggs

For the dressing:

- 1 case of old-fashioned mustard
- The juice of half an orange
- 3 cases of olive oil
- Salt pepper

PREPARATION

Prepare the dressing:

1. Dissolve mustard with orange juice.
2. Gradually add the olive oil, stirring vigorously.
3. Salt pepper.
4. Optional: add a pinch of honey.

The plate:

5. Wash, dry and clean the purslane.
6. Cut the beetroot, cooked in a pressure cooker or steamed, into small cubes.
7. Put the purslane in a salad bowl.
8. Add the chopped shallot, the cubes or slices of beetroot, then crumble the feta.
9. Peel and cut hard-boiled eggs into wedges, strips or breadcrumbs.
10. Arrange them on the salad.
11. Pour a little sauce over the salad.
12. Sprinkle with crumbled feta cheese or

Squash gnocchi

INGREDIENTS

- 1 slice of pumpkin
- 2 whole eggs
- 200g flour
- Salt
- Pepper
- Butter
- Grated parmesan or gruyere cheese

PREPARATION

1. Steam the squash in the pressure cooker or blanch it for 5 minutes.
2. Crush the pulp well in a salad bowl, season with salt and pepper.
3. Once cooled, add 2 whole eggs to this preparation.
4. Mix well. Then add the flour.
5. Boil water. Form with a teaspoon the small packets of dough which are deposited in the boiling esu.
6. When the gnocchi rise to the surface, they are cooked.
7. Arrange the gnocchi on plates, sprinkle with melted butter and Parmesan or Gruyere cheese.

Pork tenderloin generous garlic & herb cheese sauce

Preparation : 30 mins   *Ready in: 15 min*   *Portions : 4 people*

INGREDIENTS

PREPARATION

- 1 pork loin, around 450g
- 2 carrots
- 9 small potatoes
- 2 minced garlic cloves + 1 small shallot
- 1 jar of 150 g garlic and herb boursin
- 2 tablespoons light cream
- 2 teaspoons of beef broth
- 200ml of water + 50ml
- 1 pinch of salt and Espelette pepper

1. Fry the filet mignon in a little olive oil... the minced shallot... the garlic then the sliced carrots... the potatoes cut in half...
2. Salt and pepper a little Add the Espelette pepper. Let's go back for a moment.
3. Add the cheese... The fresh cream... First dilute the veal stock in 200 ml of water... Add the rest of the water... Stir gently.
4. Cook for 15 minutes in your pressure cooker or cookeo then serve hot after sprinkling with chopped parsley.

Turkey cutlets stuffed with butter-cheese-parsley and pepper

Preparation : 15 mins   Ready in: 15 min   Portions : 6 people

INGREDIENTS

PREPARATION

- 6 beautiful large turkey cutlets of 300g each, my children are big eaters.
- 100g of butter
- 200 g laughing cow cheese
- 1 small bunch of parsley
- Salt
- Ground pepper

1. Divide the cutlets.
2. Salt pepper
3. To book
4. Mix the butter, which must be very cold, with the cheese, chopped parsley, salt and pepper.
5. Make it into a paste.
6. Then generously spread this stuffing over the chops.
7. Roll them up and hold them with small wooden sticks soaked in water overnight.
8. Turn on and heat the pressure cooker or griddle.
9. Save the chops.
10. Cover and let fry at high temperature.
11. Flip and continue cooking.
12. It's best to keep the meat juicy to have that wonderful tenderness.
13. You are free to cook longer.
14. Serve with baked potatoes the same way, recipe to come

Mrouzia (Moroccan dish for very great occasions)

Preparation : 1 hour 30 minutes   **Ready in : 30 min**   **Portions : 4 people**

INGREDIENTS

- 4 pieces of leg of lamb meat.
- A big onion.
- Olive oil.
- A knob of butter.
- Salt + pepper + ginger + raz el hanout + nutmeg + turmeric (This combination of seasonings is essential to obtain this famous flavour).
- Two tablespoons of honey.
- A handful of raisins (the big raisins).
- A handful of blanched almonds.

PREPARATION

1. Put in your pan: the meat + the grated onion adds all the seasonings + the olive oil and the butter... Brown without burning... Cover with water, close your pan and cook for 30 minutes. When the meat is cooked (it must be tender) ... Open your pressure cooker add the blanched almonds washed grapes honey add a little water if necessary close your pressure cooker for 10 minutes... Open your pressure cooker again reduce the sauce. ... It must caramelize a little... Serve... and enjoy with a good glass of mint tea...

Minute quails

Preparation : 15 mins   **Servings : 8 people**

INGREDIENTS	PREPARATION

INGREDIENTS

- 8 quails
- 8 thin slices of bacon
- 75g of butter
- 1 glass of white wine
- 12 juniper berries
- 1 small glass of Armagnac
- Salt and pepper

PREPARATION

1. Quail, even farm-raised, justify flambéing them with Armagnac. Here is a menu that you can offer to your guests even if you have very little time.
2. Salt and pepper inside the quail. Wrap them with a slice of bacon and secure them with a toothpick.
3. Heat the butter in the pressure cooker put the quails in it so that they brown on all sides, add the juniper berries and the white wine and close the pressure cooker.
4. Let the valve whisper for 20 minutes; heat a metal plate to serve. Pour the Armagnac into a saucepan and heat, place the quails on the hotplate, pour the Armagnac over the quails and flambé.

Stewed beef, in sauce

Preparation : 30 mins   **Ready in : 1 hr**   **Servings : 2 people**

INGREDIENTS   ## PREPARATION

- 1 onion
- Olive oil
- 400-500g beef
- 4 carrots
- 1 red pepper
- Salt
- Cayenne pepper
- peppers
- Cumin
- Pepper
- Aromatic herbs
- 1 case of flour
- 1 beef stock cube
- About 1 liter of water

In your pressure cooker, brown the onion in the oil.
Add the beef. To mix together.
Let everything cook for a few minutes. Take a moment, book.
Replace with sliced carrots, grated pepper, stir for a few minutes.
Return the meat.
.. + Salt, cayenne pepper, paprika, cumin, pepper... Other spices according to your tastes.
To mix together.
Add the flour and the stock cube. Mix again.
(Add the potato, I take this opportunity to cook them at the same time).
Cover with water and simmer until the meat is tender...
(In the pressure cooker, 10 minutes after turning the valve, turn off the heat and cook again...
It's an electric stove... So, it still simmers a bit.)
Adjust the seasoning at the end of cooking.

Curly green cabbage smoked brisket chipolatas

Preparation : 30 mins   Ready in : 30 min   Portions : 3 people

INGREDIENTS

- 1 kale
- 1 onion
- 5 slices of smoked chicken breast
- 6 chipotles
- 15 cl of dry white wine
- 15 cl of vegetable broth
- Salt pepper

PREPARATION

1. Peel and slice the onion and chop it.
2. Strip the cabbage, devein and wash the leaves.
3. In a pressure cooker, cook the leaves with 50 cl of water for 12 minutes under pressure.
4. Drain the cabbage leaves in a colander.
5. Put oil in the bowl of the pressure cooker, add the onion, the slices of duck breast, the chipolatas.
6. And gold fairs to watch for 10 minutes.
7. Add cabbage leaves mixed with salted pepper.
8. Add the white wine, the vegetable broth.
9. Pressurize again for 15 min.

Family couscous

Preparation : 1 hour 30 minutes   **Servings : 8 people**

INGREDIENTS

- 1 lamb shoulder
- 8 chicken thighs
- 12 Merguez
- Olive oil
- 2 cans of tomato puree
- 3 tablespoons spicy couscous
- 1 teaspoon of harissa
- 2 beef stock cubes
- 3 nice tomatoes
- 10 small turnips
- 5 beautiful carrots
- 2 zucchinis
- 1 can of chickpeas
- Couscous spices, cumin

PREPARATION

1. In a pressure cooker, pour 3 tablespoons of olive oil. Put on the fire and brown the chicken thighs with the shoulder blade, when they are golden, pour the equivalent of 1 liter of water and add the cubes of beef stock, the tomato puree, the carrots, the turnips and tomatoes, couscous with spices and harissa.
2. Close your pressure cooker and count 25 minutes of cooking once the pressure rises.
3. Once the 25 minutes are up, vent the steam from your pressure cooker, open and add the zucchini and chickpeas.
4. Reheating: count 10 minutes of cooking once your pressure cooker is under pressure.
5. Cook your merguez sausages on the grill or in a pan.
6. Serve with fine grains.

Chicken couscous and merguez with a thousand flavours

Preparation : 15 mins   *Servings : 6 people*

INGREDIENTS

- 8 chicken thighs
- 9 Merguez
- 2 cans of tomato puree
- 3 tablespoons spicy couscous
- 1 teaspoon harissa, elmouth root, cumin
- 2 beef stock cubes
- 3 tomatoes
- 8 turnips
- 5 carrots
- 2 zucchinis
- 1 green and red bell pepper
- 1 can of chickpeas

PREPARATION

1. Wash and peel the carrots, turnips and tomatoes and cut them into cubes.
2. In a pressure cooker, pour 3 tablespoons of olive oil. Put on the fire and brown the chicken thighs. When they are golden brown, pour the equivalent of 1 liter of water and add the beef stock cubes, the tomato puree, the carrots, the turnips and the tomatoes, the spiced couscous and the harissa.
3. Close your pressure cooker and count 25 minutes of cooking once the pressure rises.
4. Meanwhile, wash and cut the courgettes into cubes and drain the chickpeas.
5. Once the 25 minutes are up, vent the steam from your pressure cooker, open and add the zucchini, peppers and chickpeas.
6. Reheating: count 10 minutes of cooking once your pressure cooker is under pressure.
7. Cook your merguez on a grill or in a pan, but not with the vegetables.
8. Serve with fine grains.

Pumpkin & Mushroom Soup

Preparation : 1 hour   **Ready in: 5 to 10 min**   **Servings : 6 people**

INGREDIENTS

- 1.5 kg pumpkin with nutmeg
- 300g of mushrooms
- 1 brick of semi-thick cream
- 1 bay leaf
- 3 beef bouillon cubes (1.5 litters of water)
- Salt and nutmeg

PREPARATION

1. Start by peeling the pumpkin (it's not that easy, watch your fingers!) and cut it into pieces.
2. Clean the mushrooms and cut the stems. Put everything in the pressure cooker with the bay leaf and spices. Prepare the broth and pour it over the vegetables. Close the pressure cooker and cook for 10 minutes as soon as your pressure cooker whistles.
3. Once the vegetables are cooked, mix everything together and add the liquid cream.
4. Adjust the seasoning if necessary.

Algerian Rechta with ginger

INGREDIENTS

- 1 package of fresh straight pasta
- Provide one piece of chicken per person.
- 2 turnips
- 1 large onion
- Raisins
- Salt
- Pepper
- Ginger
- Turmeric
- Olive oil
- Cinnamon sticks
- A handful of previously washed raisins

PREPARATION

1. **For the sauce:** In your pressure cooker, put the chicken and all the ingredients + the turnips + the spices Grease and let brown... Cover with water, close your pressure cooker, let cook and observe... During cooking, open, simmer then set aside. Leave enough sauce to drizzle over your pasta...
2. **Raisins:** Put on top a teaspoon of sugar + a coffee with cinnamon, bring to a simmer with a knob of butter... Set aside.
3. **For the fresh pasta:** The Rechta is prepared like a couscous with less water... In a deep bowl, open the pasta with your hands, sprinkle with a little steamed water, a couscoussier will do the trick...
4. Repeat the operation 3 times. At the end place a knob of butter on a plate as in the photo...

Pork knuckle with lentils

Preparation : 30 mins   **Servings : 6 people**

INGREDIENTS

- 1 pork knuckle of about 1 kg
- 100 g of bacon
- 2 to 3 carrots
- 1 clove of garlic
- 4-6 potatoes
- 2 boxes of lentils
- 1 onion studded with a clove
- 1 bunch of herbs
- Coarse salt, black peppercorns

PREPARATION

1. The day before for the next day
2. Put the pork knuckle in the pressure cooker, cover it with cold water, add the coarse salt,
3. The peeled onion sprinkled with cloves, the peeled carrots and the bouquet garni, about fifteen peppercorns; As soon as the valve starts to spin, leave it for about 1 hour.
   Or more if the hock requires it.
4. Once cooked, separate in two, in a container keep the shank and the filtered broth, in the second reserve the vegetables, remove the bouquet garni, the peppercorns keep everything in the refrigerator

Beef bourguignon without wine

Preparation : 2 hours　　　*Ready in : 1 hr*　　*Servings : 4 people*

INGREDIENTS

- 500 g beef bourguignon
- 2 carrots
- 3 onions
- 2 tablespoons of flour
- 3 beef bouillon cubes (1.5 litters of water)
- Thyme and bay leaf
- Salt and pepper

PREPARATION

1. Cut the meat into pieces, peel the onions and carrots. Brown the meat with a drizzle of oil, add the onions and carrots. Prepare the broth and pour the flour over the meat, cover with the broth. It should cover the meat. Add the spices and close the pressure cooker.
2. Cook for about 1 hour for tender meat and a creamy sauce.
3. For my part, I accompanied this dish with farfalle.

Quails stuffed with chestnuts and foie gras

Preparation : 15 mins   **Ready in: 45 mins**   **Portions : 2 people**

INGREDIENTS

- 4 boneless quail ready to stuff
- Foie gras
- Chestnuts

For the sauce
- Foie gras
- 10cl liquid cream
- 30g foie gras

For the chestnut purée:
- 1 kg peeled chestnuts
- 50g of butter
- 3 tablespoons fresh cream
- Salt pepper

PREPARATION

For the stuffed quail:

1. Stuff the quails by sprinkling the foie gras and pieces of chestnuts and tying them to hold them in place, melt a little duck fat in a cast iron pressure cooker, roast them for about twenty minutes, turning them frequently and basting them with bran fat.

For the foie gras sauce:

2. Heat the cream with the foie gras, it will be ready when the foie gras has melted well in the cream.

For the chestnut purée:

3. Plunge the chestnuts into boiling salted water and cook for 45 minutes or 15 minutes in a pressure cooker.

4. They are cooked when they fray easily.

5. Drain them then mix them in the blender with the butter and the fresh cream.

6. Season with salt and pepper, then reheat in a saucepan with a dash of cream just before serving.

Sausages from Montpelier and Puy lentils

Preparation : 30 mins   Ready in: 1 hr   Servings : 4 people

INGREDIENTS

- 500 g green lentils from Puy end Velay
- 4 smoked Montpelier sausages
- 1-2 carrots (depending on size)
- 1 onion
- 1 bunch of herbs

PREPARATION

1. Cut the onions into very small cubes and the peeled carrots into large rings.
2. In a pressure cooker, pour a little oil and brown the onions, then add the washed lentils, a bouquet of garnished, slices of carrots, moderate salt, pepper, put the sausage, cover with water, cook for an hour.
3. At the end of this time, remove the bouquet of garnet, rectify the spices and serve with a little parsley.

Sauerkraut garnished with New Year's Eve

Preparation : 30 mins   *Ready in : 07 min*   *Portions : 6 people*

INGREDIENTS

- 1 kg sauerkraut
- Salt and black pepper
- 2 kg Binche potatoes
- 100g salted butter
- 6 smoked cooked spare ribs
- 6 sausages
- 6 smoked sausages
- (If you wish, you can also add smoked ham or bacon)

PREPARATION

1. Peel, wash and chop the potatoes, add the sauerkraut, season with salt and pepper, smoked sausages and smoked ribs, put everything in a pressure cooker or slow cooker and cook everything together.
2. In a saucepan, put the frankfurters cut in half, cover with water and cook for 7 minutes, when your sauerkraut is cooked, remove the meat and mix the potatoes and sauerkraut well, if it is too dry, add a little cooking water. frankfurters, add the butter and mix well, add all the meats and heat through for a few minutes.

Sautéed pork stew

Preparation : 2 hours   *Ready in : 1 hr 22 min*   *Servings : 6 people*

INGREDIENTS

- 1 kg sautéed pork
- 5 beautiful carrots
- 1 beautiful leek
- 1 good stalk of celery
- 1 large onion
- Thyme
- Laurel
- 20 cl liquid fresh cream
- 60g cornstarch
- 2 egg yolks
- peppers
- Salt
- 3 cloves

PREPARATION

1. Peel the onion and stud it with cloves.
2. Peel the carrots and cut them into slices.
3. Clean the leek and celery, then cut them into two or three pieces.
4. Put everything in a pressure cooker.
5. Add the meat, thyme, bay leaf.
6. Salt, add a few peppercorns according to your taste.
7. Cover with water. Cook for 1h20 as soon as the valve turns. The meat should be tender.
8. After cooking, drain the meat and vegetables and keep warm.
9. Filter 1l of broth and add the cornstarch. Thicken.
10. Off the heat, add the eggs and cook for 2 minutes. Finish with fresh cream to give softness.
11. Pour everything over the meat and vegetables. Serve immediately hot.
12. Serve with white rice.

Tomato soup

INGREDIENTS

- 3 nice carrots
- 1 good piece of celery
- 1 onion
- A small can have crushed tomatoes
- 1 clove of garlic
- Salt and pepper
- 1 bay leaf
- Water

PREPARATION

1. Peel the carrots, cut them into slices.
2. Peel the celery and the onion, cut them into pieces.
3. Put everything in a pressure cooker with water, bay leaf, pepper and a little salt. Bake for about 15 minutes.
4. In a blender put the tomatoes, the peeled garlic, the contents of the pan (remove the bay leaf and do not put all the liquid right away).
5. Mix and all and pass through a sieve.
6. Serve hot with garlic croutons.

Toasts with beetroot pesto

Preparation : 15 mins   **Servings : 4 people**

INGREDIENTS

- 1 beet
- 20 Fines
- 1 small clove of garlic
- Olive oil
- Balsamic vinegar
- 1 lemon
- 1 egg
- Rocket salad
- soft bread

PREPARATION

1. Cook a hard-boiled egg.
2. Prepare a beetroot pesto (previously cooked in a pressure cooker): mix the beetroot, almonds, garlic, olive oil and salt.
3. Add to this base 1 can of balsamic vinegar and 1 teaspoon of lemon juice.
4. Toast your slices of bread then spread pesto, an arugula leaf and finish with a slice of hard-boiled egg.

Large White Beans with Cilantro

Preparation : 30 mins **Ready in : 30 min** **Portions : 6 people**

INGREDIENTS

- 500g beef
- 300g large white beans
- 4 garlic cloves
- 1/2 bunch coriander
- 1 onion
- 50 cl of tomato coulis
- meat broth

PREPARATION

1. Brown together the veal cut into small pieces and the chopped onion.
2. Then add 2 cloves of minced garlic, half of the chopped cilantro, the beans (purchased fresh then frozen) and the coulis. Cover with beef broth, season with salt and pepper and cook in the pressure cooker for 30 minutes.
3. In a skillet, sauté the two remaining cloves of garlic (crushed) and the remaining chopped cilantro in a generous amount of olive oil.
4. Add to beans/meat and serve.

Pasta from our family

INGREDIENTS

PREPARATION

For the broth:
- 1 leek
- 1 fennel bulb
- 2 carrots
- Parsley
- 1 rosemary
- 2 bay leaves
- 1 chicken stock cube
- Salt

For the pasta:
- 6 thin slices of Parma ham or Grisons meat
- 130g heavy cream
- 100g gorgonzola
- 1 egg yolk
- 500 g dough of your choice (I used colour)
- Chives and salt and pepper

1. Wash the leek and cut it into rings, cut the fennel pieces and cut the heart into small cubes. Peel the carrots and also cut them into cubes. Put everything in a pressure cooker with the stock cube, pour 1 liter of water and salt. Cook everything for 10 minutes. Filter the broth.

2. Cut Grisons meat or Parma ham into strips. Pour 50 cl of broth into a saucepan and reduce by about half. Add the cream and the chopped gorgonzola. Cook over low heat, when the sauce has reduced, beat the egg yolk and add it to the sauce. Allow to thicken, stirring constantly, remove from the heat and season lightly.

3. Cook the pasta as on the package. About 10 min after boiling the water. Drain them and mix them with the cream. Present in bowls, then place the strips of meat and chives on top of the filling. Serve hot.

Vinegar rice for sushi

Preparation : 15 mins   *Ready in: 20 mins*   *Portions : 4 people*

INGREDIENTS

- 300g round white rice (about 2 cups)
- Water to cook the rice (depending on the pressure cooker)

For the vinegar
- 50 ml rice vinegar or white vinegar
- 1 and 1/2 tablespoons of sugar
- 1 teaspoon of salt

PREPARATION

1. Prepare the cooked rice with a little less water. If you have the "Konbu", put it on.
2. While the rice is cooking, prepare the vinegar. Put the vinegar ingredients in a small saucepan.
3. Bring to a boil until the sugar and salt dissolve. Let cool.
4. Put the hot cooked rice in a large bowl.
5. Gradually add the vinegar to the rice while stirring. Be careful not to crush the rice!
6. Cool the rice with a fan, if you don't have one, use it while stirring the rice.
7. Cover the bowl with the damp cloth until the Maki is made.

Stewed beef à la Provencal

Preparation : 15 mins   Ready in: 30 min   Portions : 4 people

INGREDIENTS

PREPARATION

- 800 g chuck and neck of beef
- 2 sweet onions
- 2 cloves garlic
- 1 bunch of herbs
- 2 tablespoons of flour
- 50 cl of white wine
- 1 can of peeled tomatoes
- 30 pitted olives
- 1 whole Basque pepper without seeds.
- 1 tablespoon olive oil
- Salt and pepper

1. Brown the meat in olive oil.
2. Add the chopped onions, brown and sprinkle with flour. Mix well.
3. Top with white wine, tomatoes, crushed garlic, olives, bouquet garni and pepper. Salt and pepper.
4. Mix well
5. Close the pressure cooker and count 30 to 35 minutes from the whispering of the tap.
6. Serve with potatoes or pasta.

Morteau sausage with green lentils and old-fashioned mustard

Preparation : 30 mins   **Ready in: 25 min**   **Portions : 3 people**

INGREDIENTS

- 300g green lentils
- 2 red onions
- 2 sand carrots
- 1/2 beef cube
- 1 sachet of Knorr bouquet garni
- 1 Morteau sausage (the gold medal)
- 4 heaping tablespoons old-fashioned mustard
- 2 tablespoons olive oil
- 750ml water

PREPARATION

1. Cut the red onions, sauté them in olive oil.
2. Add the diced carrots, sauté 3-4 minutes in the onions.
3. Put the half cube of old-fashioned mustard and a sachet of Knorr's bouquet garni
4. Fill the pressure cooker with approximately 750 ml of cold water
5. Place the Morteau sausage without perforating it in the lentils and season with pepper, no need to add salt.
6. Cook in the pressure cooker for about twenty minutes, the cooking time depends on the quality of the lentils.
7. Cut the sausage into small or large slices and enjoy

Toulouse sausages with white beans

Preparation : 30 mins   **Ready in + : 40 min**   **Portions : 4 people**

INGREDIENTS

- 250 g white beans ingot
- 8 smoked sausages
- 200g smoked bacon
- 2 onions
- 3 cloves of garlic
- 40 cl of chicken broth
- 3 carrots
- 2 cans of flour
- Pepper

PREPARATION

1. Soak the beans overnight.
2. The next day, rinse them with cold water.
3. In a pressure cooker put the bacon onions the minced garlic.
4. Remove them, add the sausages and brown them a little.
5. Peel the carrots and cut them into rings, add them to the rest of the ingredients.
6. Add a little broth stir put the flour mixture.
7. Add the beans, the rest of the broth should cover the beans.
8. Season with pepper
9. Close the lid and pressurize for 40 minutes.

Tuberous parsley soup

Preparation : 15 mins   Ready in + : 30 min   Portions : 4 people

INGREDIENTS

PREPARATION

- 2 parsley tubers
- 1 white leek
- 1 onion
- 1 knob of butter
- 1 point
- 1 vegetable stock cube
- 1 chicken stock cube
- 1 -1 1/2 litters of water
- Salt pepper

1. Wash, peel the vegetables.
2. Cut them into big chunks.
3. Fry the onion and leek without colouring in a little fat.
4. Add the parsley tubers, potato.
5. Crumble the stock cubes.
6. Pepper (salt the cubes a little when they are already salty).
7. Pour water to the top and cook covered.
8. For me, 10 min in the pressure cooker (30 min in the pan).
9. Mixer.
10. To taste lengthen with a little water (or with milk or cream), season again if necessary.
11. When serving, why not present it with croutons, grilled smoked sausages, seeds...?

Velouté of vegetables with strips of grilled peppers

Preparation : 15 mins   **Ready in: 40 min**   **Portions : 4 people**

INGREDIENTS	PREPARATION

INGREDIENTS

- 1 yellow bell pepper
- 1/2 butternut squash
- 1 leek
- 3 carrots
- 2 zucchinis
- 2 potatoes
- 1 tomato
- 1 onion
- 1 stock cube
- 10 cl fresh cream
- Butter
- 1 red pepper
- Croutons
- Parmesan cheese

PREPARATION

1. Peel, wash and cut the vegetables into small pieces.
2. Brown the leek in the butter for about 10 minutes and set aside.
3. Cut the peppers into strips and roast them in a pan with a drizzle of olive oil.
4. Cut the pieces of bread into cubes and toast them.
5. Put the other vegetables in a saucepan and cover them with water, with half the stock cube and cook for 30 minutes or 10 minutes in the pressure cooker.
6. Cover the leek with water and add the rest of the broth, cook for about 20 minutes.
7. When the vegetables are cooked, mash them (without the leeks) and season with salt and pepper to taste.
8. Add the fresh cream and the leek without mixing.
9. Serve on plates sprinkled with croutons, pepper strips and parmesan cheese.

Cauliflower gratin with coconut milk and curry

Preparation : 15 mins   *Ready in: 30 min*   *Portions : 4 people*

INGREDIENTS

- 1 cauliflower
- 20 cl of coconut milk
- 10 cl whipped cream
- 3 eggs
- 1 heaping tbsp curry powder
- 1 teaspoon Sriracha sauce (or pinch of chilli) optional ingredient
- 1 pinch of salt
- 2 handfuls of grated cheese

PREPARATION

1. Remove the leaves and the heart of the cauliflower, cut it into florets, wash it and cook it for 10 minutes in a pressure cooker or simply in a saucepan.
2. Arrange your cauliflower florets in a gratin dish.
3. In a bowl, beat the eggs and add the coconut milk, cream, curry, Salt and Sriracha sauce or pepper in place of the chilli or sauce.
4. Sprinkle with grated cheese.
5. Pour over the cauliflower and bake in a preheated oven at 180°C for 30 to 35 minutes.

Sauerkraut

Preparation : 45 mins   Ready in : 45 mins   Portions : 4 people

INGREDIENTS

- 1 kg 500 g raw sauerkraut
- 100g lard
- 1 carrot
- 1 onion studded with 5 cloves
- 4 slices of cooked chicken breast
- 1 Morteau sausage
- 4 small metkas
- 2 melons and 4 "sosiski" or Strasbourg sausages. 50cl of white wine from Alsace
- 2 bay leaves
- Salt and pepper and the juice of 1/2 lemon "for the acidity of the cabbage"

PREPARATION

1. Blanch the sauerkraut: plunge it into a large saucepan of boiling water, as soon as it foams, remove it from the heat, drain it, run it under cold water and squeeze it between your hands to remove the water. In your pressure cooker, place the carrot cut in 2, the onion studded with cloves and the cooked duck breast, then half the sauerkraut, salt and pepper. Arrange the sausage cut into slices, the chopped "metka" and "melona", the butter in small pieces.

2. Cover with the rest of the cabbage, salt and pepper again, pour in the white wine and the juice of 1/2 lemon. Close the pressure cooker, increase the pressure to high heat, then put on low heat and cook for 45 minutes. at 1 o'clock

3. For the "sosiski" or "Strasbourg" sausages, prick them and immerse them for a few minutes in a pan of boiling water, then drain them. Serve hot with a boiled potato.

Beef rolls with onions

Preparation : 30 mins   **Ready in : 30 min**   **Portions : 6 people**

INGREDIENTS

- 6 slices of beefsteak thin and wide
- A little flour
- 25g of butter
- 1 tablespoon oil
- 2 medium onions
- 2 cloves garlic
- Sprig of aromatic herbs
- Salt and pepper
- 1 1/2 glass of white or red wine
- 1/2 teaspoon of tomato coffee concentrate.

For the stuffing:
- 200g chorizo meat
- 1 shallot, chopped
- Chopped parsley
- Salt
- Pepper
- 2 pinches of nutmeg
- 1 egg
- 1 tablespoon of breadcrumbs
- Fine kitchen twine

PREPARATION

1. Mix all the ingredients together.
2. Spread a quarter over each steak.
3. Roll them into paupiettes and tie them in the shape of a cross.
4. Flour them very lightly.
5. Heat the butter and oil well in the pressure cooker.
6. Brown the paupiettes on all sides.
7. Halfway through cooking, add the chopped onions.
8. When they are coloured in turn, add the crushed garlic, the bouquet garni, salt and pepper.
9. Sprinkle with the wine in which the tomato paste has been dissolved.
10. Close the pressure cooker.
11. Cook very gently for 30 minutes from the pressure setting.
12. Serve the veal rolls drizzled with the sauce removed from the bouquet garni.
13. Serve with rice, pasta or potato.

Sautéed hunter's veal

Preparation : 15 mins   **Ready in : 2 hrs**   **Servings : 4 people**

INGREDIENTS

- 1 kg 700 of sautéed beef
- 500g mushrooms
- 4 shallots
- 7 carrots
- 6 tomatoes
- 2 glasses of dry white wine
- 1 tablespoon of tomato puree
- 2 tablespoons olive oil
- 2 cloves garlic
- Basil, chopped parsley
- Salt pepper

PREPARATION

1. Pour the oil into the pan or pressure cooker and brown the meat cut into pieces.
2. until golden brown on all sides.
3. Add the peeled and chopped shallots, the peeled and chopped carrots, diced tomatoes, frozen straight mushrooms,
4. White wine, peeled and chopped garlic, herbs, seasoning.
5. Cover and simmer for about 1h30 over low heat or in a pressure cooker; then the time will be reduced, count 30 minutes from the rotation of the valve.
6. Note that there is not much sauce and the meat is very tender.

Simple appetizers to make

Preparation : 30 mins   Servings : 4 people

INGREDIENTS

- 1/4 cucumber
- 2 potatoes (not small) 2 slices of smoked salmon or trout
- 4 mozzarella balls
- 4 cherry tomatoes (garnish)
- 2 boiled eggs
- Mayo (homemade or ready-made)
- 1/2 can of tuna

PREPARATION

1. Cook hard-boiled eggs. Cook the potatoes whole (avoid boiling) or sliced in a pressure cooker (6 mm thick) Make homemade mayonnaise (egg yolk + 1 tablespoon mustard, seasoning, oil). Cut into slices (about 1 cm)

2. Salmon trout, eye, crumbles easily by rolling the mozzarella strips, surrounding the mozzarella balls again

3. Mix a hard-boiled egg (cooled) and the wheat from the 2nd egg + mayonnaise and tuna and in a piping bag for easy dressing

4. Using a cookie cutter, cut the potatoes (previously cut into rounds of about 6 mm, otherwise with a pressure cooker) prepare as in the photo above.

5. Decorate with a crumb of egg yolk for the salmon. - cucumber, and crown with a cherry tomato for potato and hard-boiled egg tuna-mayonnaise.

Stuffed roasted pork

Preparation : 30 mins   **Ready in : 50 min**   **Portions : 6 people**

INGREDIENTS

PREPARATION

- Roast pork, about 500 g,
- Salt pepper,
- 2 slices of smoked ham,
- Slices of fresh tomato,
- 1 onion,
- A knob of butter,
- Provencal herbs,
- Thyme,
- 20 cl of liquid (wine, beer, water, broth)

1. Cut the pork roast in half lengthwise.
2. Open it, salt and pepper.
3. Arrange the slices of smoked ham.
4. You can according to taste and desire, also put tomatoes, slices of cheese, onion,
5. Place 2 slices of bacon on top.
6. Close the roast and tie it carefully.
7. Sprinkle with Herbs of Provence.
8. Melt a knob of butter in the pressure cooker (or casserole dish).
9. Brown the roast in it.
10. Salt pepper,
11. Add a large chopped onion, 20 cl of red wine (this time),
12. Season with herbs de Provence, thyme, and other condiments according to taste and desire.
13. Cook for about 10 min (when the valve 'whistle'), about 30-35 min in a saucepan.
14. Turn off the heat source and let close for another 5 minutes.
15. For the pressure cooker, release the steam, open the pan.
16. The roast should be golden brown.
17. Check for doneness by lightly cutting the inside with a knife.

Lemon chicken couscous

Preparation : 15 mins   **Ready in : 25 min**   **Portions : 4 people**

INGREDIENTS

- 8 chicken thighs
- 2 cans of tomato puree
- 3 tablespoons spicy couscous
- 1 teaspoon harissa, elmouth root, cumin
- 3 tomatoes
- 2 turnips
- 5 carrots
- 2 zucchinis
- 1 green and red bell pepper
- 1 can of chickpeas
- A lemon juices
- 1 lemon cut into wedges

PREPARATION

1. In a pressure cooker, pour 3 tablespoons of olive oil. Put the fire with a little spice and brown the chicken when it is well browned, add the vegetables, the tomato puree, the spicy couscous and the harissa with the juice and the pieces of lemon.
2. Cover with water, close the pressure cooker and cook for 25 minutes once the pressure has risen.
3. When the 25 minutes are up, release the steam from your pressure cooker, open and add the chickpeas.
4. Reheating: count 10 minutes of cooking once your pressure cooker is under pressure.
5. Serve with fine grains.

Braised pork cheeks with porcini mushrooms

Preparation : 45 mins **Ready in : 05 min** **Portions : 3 people**

INGREDIENTS

- 6 boneless pork cheeks 600/700 g
- 40g dried porcini mushrooms
- 3 carrots about 300 g
- 2 onions of about 100 g
- 3 crushed garlics
- 1 tbsp parsley
- 100g pitted green olives
- 3 tablespoons oil
- 1 tablespoon of tomato puree
- 250ml beef stock
- Salt and pepper
- 125ml dry white wine

PREPARATION

1. Put the porcini mushrooms to be rehydrated in water, clean the carrots and cut them into rings, cut the onions.

2. In a pressure cooker, pour the oil and brown each cheek on both sides, then add the parsley, the onion, the peeled and germ-free garlic and the crushed garlic, leave to stand for 5 minutes, then add the tomato puree, can be removed with dried white wine.

3. Put back the cheeks and 250 ml of veal stock, season with salt and pepper and close the pressure cooker as soon as the valve is turned, count 20 minutes and add the green olives and the drained mushrooms, when the valve is again in rotation, lower the pressure. gas and count 20 minutes maximum serve with steamed potatoes or the desired starch.

Ricotta carrot puree

Preparation : 15 mins   **Ready in: 15 min**   **Portions : 3 people**

INGREDIENTS

- A dozen carrots
- 3 large potatoes
- 150g ricotta
- Salt pepper
- Herbs of your choice (optional, I added chives)
- Milk or cream if needed

PREPARATION

1. Peel your carrots and potatoes, wash the potatoes under the tap. Cook everything in a pressure cooker for about 15 minutes. Mix with the ricotta and if necessary, milk or cream, salt, pepper (herbs) and mix again! Here it is ready! You can heat it up in the microwave! It's fast and very good!

Broccoli cheese mousse

Preparation : 15 mins   **Ready in: 20 mins**   **Portions : 3 people**

INGREDIENTS

- 3 small bunches of broccolis
- 1 natural yoghurt (velvety type)
- 10cl of cream
- 2 laughing cow
- 2 servings of walnut tartare
- 2 eggs
- Salt pepper
- Parmesan cheese

PREPARATION

1. Cut your broccoli into small bouquets, put them in water to clean them. Cook them in a pressure cooker for 10_15 minutes.
2. Beat the eggs with the yoghurt and cream. Add the laughing cow and walnut tartare portions, season with salt and pepper and mix well. (You can add aromatic or other herbs...).
3. Drain the broccoli florets and mix. Add them to the preparation and mix well, sprinkle generously with parmesan before baking. 6 for about 15-20 minutes.

Zucchini, Mushroom and Raclette Gratin

Preparation : 15 mins   **Ready in : 40 min**   **Portions : 3 people**

INGREDIENTS

- 5 zucchinis
- 100g of mushrooms
- 1 handful of dried porcini mushrooms
- 1 handful of dried trumpets of death
- 200g raclette cheese (with pepper for me)
- Salt, pepper, Provence herbs (or others)
- 20g of butter
- 25cl of milk
- A little flour

PREPARATION

1. We start by boiling water, add chopped dried mushrooms and turn off the heat, leave for about 10 minutes.
2. Peel the courgettes (you can cook them for 10 minutes in a pressure cooker if you wish), cut them into small cubes and place them in a gratin dish.
3. Add the previously cleaned and chopped mushrooms.
4. Make a small bechamel sauce by melting the butter, add a dollop of flour and the milk little by little while mixing, melt 100 g of raclette cheese.
5. Pass the dried mushrooms through a sieve and add them to the béchamel sauce, salt and pepper and add everything to the gratin dish, sprinkle with Provencal herbs, mix and cut the rest of the cheese into cubes.

Eggplant stuffed with buckwheat seeds

Preparation : 15 mins   **Ready in : 5 to 10 min**   **Servings : 2 people**

INGREDIENTS	PREPARATION

INGREDIENTS

- 1 eggplant
- 1 glass of raw buckwheat seeds
- 2 tomatoes
- 1 shallot
- Salt
- Parsley

PREPARATION

1. Cut the eggplant in half lengthwise and scoop out the pulp. Book.
2. Boil the buckwheat in water. Book.
3. In the pressure cooker, cook the eggplants.
4. Cut the tomatoes into cubes, the onion and pass through a food processor with the tomato pulp.
5. Pour the vegetable filling into a saucepan and cook for 10 minutes. Add the buckwheat seeds and mix.
6. Fill the aubergines with the stuffing.

Tuna and potato terrine

Preparation : 45 mins   **Ready in : 5 to 10 min**   **Servings : 6 people**

INGREDIENTS

- 4 large potatoes.
- 5 tablespoons of mayonnaise.
- 3 hard-boiled eggs
- 1 can of tuna of 250 g
- Salt pepper

PREPARATION

1. Cook the potatoes with the skin in boiling water or in a pressure cooker.
2. Cook hard-boiled eggs. (10 minutes after boiling the water).
3. Peel the hot potatoes and mash them with a fork. Mix them delicately with the mayonnaise, the hard-boiled eggs in pieces and the shredded tuna.
4. Line a mold with aluminium or transparent paper.
5. Pour the preparation and cover the top with the paper that protrudes from the edge.
6. Put in the refrigerator for at least 5 hours.
7. Gently unmould.
8. Serve with a salad, pickles and aioli sauce or ketchup.

Pumpkin gnocchi

Preparation : 1 hour   **Ready in : 15 min**   **Portions : 4 people**

INGREDIENTS

PREPARATION

- 500g of squash
- 100g of butter
- 125g flour
- 4 eggs
- 100 g grated Gruyere cheese + 50 g (garnish)
- 10 cl fresh cream
- Salt
- Pepper
- Nutmeg powder
- Olive oil

1. Peel and seed the pumpkin, cut it into cubes and cook it in salted water in a pressure cooker for 10 to 15 minutes.
2. Drain and pass through a vegetable mill.
3. Put this puree in a saucepan and cook over low heat.
4. Add the butter, then the flour, mix until a paste comes away from the pan.
5. Off the heat, add the eggs, grated Gruyere, salt, pepper, sprinkle with nutmeg and mix well.
6. Boil salted water in a saucepan with a drizzle of olive oil.
7. Preheat the oven on grill mode.
8. Using a pastry bag, form small meatballs and immerse them in boiling water.
9. Remove the gnocchi with a slotted spoon as soon as they rise to the surface.
10. Cover the gnocchi with fresh cream, season with salt and pepper, sprinkle with grated cheese and grill for 5 minutes.

Sardines in casserole dish

Preparation : 15 mins   **Ready in : 15 min**   **Portions : 4 people**

INGREDIENTS

- 600g sardines
- 15 cl of olive oil
- 8 cl of vinegar
- 2 bay leaves
- 4 nails
- 1/2 teaspoon of salt
- 1 red or green bell pepper, sliced
- 4 tablespoons of water

PREPARATION

1. Put the sardines in a pressure cooker, add all the ingredients, close the pan and cook for 10-15 minutes (from boiling). The sardines will be ready when the vinegar and water have evaporated.
2. In a serving dish, arrange the sardines with the pepper rings, drizzle with the cooking juices.

Stuffed with small vegetables

Preparation : 30 mins   *Ready in _ : 1 hr Servings : 6 people*

INGREDIENTS

- 6 large "Macao or calico" artichokes
- 2 large onions
- 4 large pompadour potatoes
- 2 nice tomatoes
- 700 G Side of your choice: Pork
- OR veal-pork OR veal-pork
- 1 tablespoon of oregano
- 1 tablespoon beef broth
- 2 garlic - parsley
- Salt pepper,
- Olive oil

PREPARATION

1. In the pressure cooker, pre-cook the potatoes with their skin on, do the same with the unpeeled onions and the artichokes, of which only the lower part will remain, leave to cool
2. Mix with the garnish of your choice, salt, pepper, oregano, beef broth, minced garlic and parsley.
3. Peel the potatoes and core them, peel the onions and press them into the heart, remove the tomatoes and thin the artichokes, stuff each vegetable and place them in the baking dish.
4. Drizzle with olive oil and bake until toppings are browned, 1 hour.
5. You can sprinkle with breadcrumbs halfway through cooking.
6. Serve on the same plate.
7. The pieces of potato that I take out I interpose them in the vegetables.

Pan - fried green beans, tomatoes, potatoes and tomatoes with bacon bits

---

Preparation : 30 mins   **Ready in : 40 min**   **Portions : 2 people**

INGREDIENTS

PREPARATION

- 1 onion
- 1 clove of garlic
- 1mg walnuts
- 4 potatoes
- 250g fresh green beans
- 100g bacon (smoked for me)
- 1 large tomato
- Salt
- Pepper
- A few cumin seeds
- Parsley

1. Wash, peel, cut the potatoes into pieces. Cook them in salted water.
2. Remove the green beans and cook them in a saucepan/pressure cooker in salted boiling water.
3. Drain.
4. After about 10 minutes of cooking, I let the steam through and watch the paddles to watch the potatoes cook before draining the water (and continuing to cook if necessary).
5. Peel, chop the onion and the clove of garlic.
6. Brown them with a knob of butter in a large skillet.
7. Sprinkle with 1 good pinch of turmeric.
8. Gradually add the bacon bits, tomato pieces, green beans.
9. Salt pepper.
10. Add some cumin seeds.
11. Cook for a few more minutes over low heat.
12. Mix gently so as not to break up the vegetables too much.
13. Sprinkle with parsley and serve.

Pistou soup

Preparation : 1 hour   Ready in : 1 hr   Servings : 4 people

INGREDIENTS

PREPARATION

For the soup:
- 150g red beans
- 150 g white beans
- 150g green beans
- 2 fresh tomatoes, diced
- 1/2 can of crushed tomatoes
- 150 g small lead paste
- 1 vegetable stock cube (optional)
- Salt pepper.

For the pesto:
- 1 basil bush
- 20 to 30 cl of olive oil
- 50g pine nuts (or walnuts or almonds)
- 2 cloves garlic
- 50g of parmesan
- Salt pepper

1. Soak dry beans, white and red, in water for at least 3 hours. But the ideal is the day before for the next day. At the end of this soaking period, drain and rinse.
2. If you buy your beans canned, of course you have to skip this step as they are pre-cooked.
3. In a pressure cooker (the cookeo for me), put the green beans cut into 2 or 3 pieces, the white and red beans and the rest of the ingredients except the pasta and cover with water (about 2 litters). Cook under pressure for 45 minutes, then open the appliance and place the pasta in it. Pressure cook again for 10 minutes.
4. If you use a simple pot, allow 2 hours of cooking over medium heat and put the pasta 15 minutes before the end of cooking.
5. While the soup is cooking, prepare the pesto.
6. Peel all the basil and rinse the leaves.
7. Mix all the ingredients in a blender.
8. If you use almonds like me, I soak them 1 hour before in water then I peel them before mixing them with the rest of the ingredients.
9. Add the pesto to the soup just before serving.

Carrot and turnip hotpot

Preparation : 15 mins **Ready in : 15 min** **Portions : 2 people**

INGREDIENTS

- 1/2 kilo of carrot
- 2-3 turnips
- 3-4 potatoes
- 1 small onion
- 1 bay leaf
- 1 sprig of thyme
- 1 knob of butter
- 1/2 glass of water

PREPARATION

1. Wash, peel the potatoes, carrots and turnips.
2. Cut them into pieces.
3. Cook them for 10 minutes in a little salted water (or leftover vegetable broth) in a pressure cooker.
4. ! Do not dip them in juice!
5. Peel the onion and cut it into small pieces.
6. Brown it in the butter in a large saucepan with the sausages.
7. Drain the vegetables.
8. Add the sautéed onion with the sausage.
9. Shred it all up (I like to leave a few big chunks in there).
10. Serve with the chorizo and accompany the stew with 1 tablespoon of mustard.

Guinea fowl legs stewed with green lentils

Preparation : 15 mins   *Ready in: 40 min*   *Portions : 2 people*

INGREDIENTS

- 4 guinea fowl legs
- 240g green lentils
- 2 carrots
- 1 small onion
- 1/2 stalk of celery
- 100 g of bacon
- 1 sprig of thyme 1 bay leaf
- 1/2 chicken stock cube
- Pepper

PREPARATION

1. Brown the guinea fowl in a pressure cooker or pot in a teaspoon of olive oil... the chopped onion... the bacon... then... the sliced carrots... the branch of celery... Turn everything over for 3 minutes then pour a glass of water... Add the diced pepper to the bouquet garni.
2. I chose to cook the thighs and these vegetables a little in advance for 10 minutes.
3. Once the first cooking is finished, cover everything again with cold water and add the lentils for a cooking time of 30 minutes.
4. Lentils take on the taste of guinea fowl!

Pea pod soup

Preparation : 40 mins   *Servings : 4 people*

INGREDIENTS

- 200-250g pea pods
- 1 medium zucchini
- 1-2 potatoes
- 1 medium onion
- 2 litters of water
- Salt
- Pepper
- 1 vegetable stock cube
- Parsley (optional).

PREPARATION

1. Remove the fillets from the pods, wash them, then put them in the side dish with the onion, zucchini, potatoes cleaned and cut into pieces.
2. Add salt, pepper and stock cube.
3. Cover with 2 litters of water.
4. Put in the pressure cooker Cook 12 min after the start of the pressure (40 min in a normal saucepan).
5. Optionally add parsley at the end of cooking.
6. When the soup is finished, blend it then pass it through a colander to remove the rest of the fillets, pressing well to extract all the liquid.
7. You can accompany this soup with cream/milk, fried croutons, smoked bacon, ... mint, basil...
8. Or with 1 poached egg (per person), crushed hard, ...

Salmon and leek pasta

Preparation : 30 mins   **Ready in: 30 min**   **Portions : 3 people**

INGREDIENTS

- 300g pasta
- 2 white leeks
- 4 fresh salmon fillets (600g)
- 1 shallot
- 1 chicken stock cube
- 330ml cream
- 1 tablespoon Sriracha sauce (optional)
- 1 pinch of salt and ground pepper

PREPARATION

1. Remove the stem and green leaves from the leeks and carefully clean the whites. Cut them into 3 sections and cook them for 10 minutes in the pressure cooker. Set aside and when they have cooled, cut them into strips.
2. Remove the skin from the salmon fillets and cut the meat into cubes about 1.5 cm on each side.
3. Peel and finely chop the shallot. Put the cubes obtained in a saucepan, add the white wine and the crumbled chicken stock cube. Cook until there are only about 2 tablespoons of liquid left in the pan (about ten minutes over high heat). Pour this mixture into a saucepan. To book.
4. Cook the pasta.
5. When there are only 5 minutes left to cook the pasta, pour the cream into the pan where you had put the rest of the white wine and the shallot, add the Sriracha sauce. Bring to a boil and add the salmon pieces and leeks. Leave to cook for a few minutes, until the fish cooks and the leeks heat up.
6. Add the cooked pasta and mix well.

Catalan - style veal sauté

Preparation : 45 mins   **Ready in : 5 to 10 min**   **Servings : 6 people**

INGREDIENTS

- 1Kg 500 of sautéed beef
- 1 kg of potatoes
- 150g sausage
- 3 tomatoes
- 2 onions
- 3 cloves of garlic
- 30 green olives
- 2 tablespoons oil
- 15 cl dry white wine or water
- Salt pepper

PREPARATION

1. Flour the pieces of meat cut into large cubes and brown them in oil, add the chopped onion and garlic, sprinkle with dry white wine then put the tomatoes without seeds and peeled (thawed) or canned if you don't have one.
2. Salt and pepper lightly and cook for 10 minutes as soon as you turn the valve.
3. Meanwhile, peel and cut the potatoes into quarters, chop the chorizo and rinse the green olives.
4. Open the pressure cooker, add the potatoes, olives, chorizo, adjust the seasoning if necessary and put back for about 15 minutes until cooked.
5. You can serve immediately.

Tagine veal tomato

Preparation : 15 mins　　　　**Servings : 4 people**

INGREDIENTS

- Provide 1 piece of meat per person
- 1 onion
- 3 extra ripe tomatoes
- Garlic
- Olive oil
- sweet paprika
- Pepper
- Ginger
- Salt

PREPARATION

1. Brown the onion, meat, spices, oil, garlic in the pressure cooker... Add the tomatoes. Cover... Close your pressure cooker... Check the cooking of the meat, reduce the sauce to your liking... Serve with a salad.
2. PS you can add olives and candied lemon at the end

Stuffed chicory

Preparation : 30 mins   Ready in: 30 min   Portions : 3 people

INGREDIENTS

PREPARATION

- 6 fine endives
- 200g minced pork
- 200g ground beef
- 1 onion
- 1 egg
- Salt
- Pepper
- Parsley
- Butter

1. The day before, blanch the endives for 10 minutes in the pressure cooker and drain.
2. The next day, in a salad bowl, mix the meat with the chopped onion, whole egg, salt, pepper and parsley.
3. Separate your endives to make trays, making sure there is a bottom on the left, then decorate with the garnish, arrange them in a buttered gratin dish and bake in a hot oven at 180° for 25 to 30 minutes.

Coconut Cauliflower

Preparation : 15 mins	Ready in: 20 mins	Portions : 3 people

INGREDIENTS

- 1 cauliflower
- 2 tablespoons of flour
- Spices to taste (I used curry and sweet pepper)
- 42cl of coconut milk (a whole can)
- 1 tablespoon lemon juice
- Salt

PREPARATION

1. Wash, cut the cauliflower into small pieces and cook in the pressure cooker for about 10 minutes.
2. In a bowl mix the flour and spices. Then add salt and dissolve in 15 cl of water. To book.
3. When the cauliflower is cooked, put it in a saucepan with the coconut milk and cook over low heat for 5 minutes. Salt, pepper and add the lemon juice while mixing.
4. Then add the spice preparation while mixing.
5. Cook for a few more minutes and voila!

Tomato/coconut beans

Preparation : 15 mins　　　*Ready in : 15 min*　　　*Portions : 3 people*

INGREDIENTS

- 500g green beans
- 100 g of bacon
- 4 tomatoes
- 10cl coconut milk
- 1 can of tomato sauce in a tube
- Herbs of your choice

PREPARATION

1. Cook the green beans in a pressure cooker for about 10 minutes.
2. In a hot skillet, cook the bacon for 5 minutes over low heat, add the tomatoes mixed with the tomato sauce with the coconut milk and the cooked green beans.
3. Add some herbs and heat for a few minutes over low heat.

Chilli con carne pasta gratin

Preparation : 15 mins   Ready in : 05 min   Portions : 3 people

INGREDIENTS

- 150g pasta
- 100 beans
- 295 g minced beef in very small pieces
- 1 onion
- 2 cloves garlic
- 1 red pepper
- 1 can of peeled tomatoes
- Salt, pepper, spices (sweet peppers and paprika powder)
- Olive oil
- Grated cheese

PREPARATION

1. In a pressure cooker, cook the red beans in 3 times their volume of water for about 30 minutes.
2. Meanwhile, cook the pasta in salted water over high heat for about 4/5 minutes.
3. In a skillet, brown the onion, the minced garlic in a little olive oil, add the diced pepper, the minced meat, the peeled tomatoes, salt and pepper.
4. In an ovenproof dish, put the pasta, the red beans and the mixture (meat, pepper...).
5. Generously add the grated cheese.
6. And we put it in the oven under the broiler until the cheese melts.

Ratatouille

INGREDIENTS

- 700g chicken fillet
- 4 tomatoes (or peeled tomatoes)
- 5 zucchini
- 4 large potatoes
- 1 large eggplant
- 3 red peppers
- Tomato sauce
- White wine
- Salt pepper
- Spices (Provence herbs, fine herbs, basil, curry, sweet pepper as desired)

PREPARATION

1. Peel and cut the vegetables into pieces (the size you prefer) Except the tomatoes.

2. Cook the tomatoes in the pressure cooker for 5 minutes. Meanwhile, cut the chicken into pieces, cook it in olive oil, add the tomato sauce (quantity of your choice), finally add the white wine.

3. Wait a bit and add the vegetables. When the tomatoes are cooked, peel them and add them to the pan, mix, salt, pepper, season a lot and mix again, marinate for a good 2 hours (the longer the better)

Pumpkin, chestnut and apple velouté

Preparation : 45 mins   *Ready in : 45 mins*   *Portions : 6 people*

INGREDIENTS

- 800 g pumpkin in pieces
- 350 to 400 g chestnuts in a jar
- 2 golden apples
- 150g smoked bacon
- 1/4 liter of water + 1/4 liter of milk
- 200 ml light liquid cream
- 20g of butter
- Salt
- Pepper

PREPARATION

1. Melt the butter in a saucepan, sear the bacon bits to brown, drain and set aside.
2. In place of the bacon bits, put the pieces of pumpkin and the peeled and quartered apples
3. Cook 5 minutes.
4. Reserve 5 or 6 chestnuts for the dishes and add the rest to the pumpkin
5. Add water, milk, salt, pepper.
6. Close and cook for 40 min (25 in a pressure cooker!)
7. Mix the velouté with the cream, add the bacon bits.
8. Serve very hot with broken chestnuts, small garlic croutons, a small dab of cream.
9. For lovers of parmesan or grated Emmental!

Homemade Sushis and Makis

Preparation : 30 mins   **Ready in: 20 mins**   **Portions : 6 people**

INGREDIENTS

- 2 cups of sushi rice
- A few slices of smoked salmon
- 1 omelette composed of 3 eggs
- 1 small piece of eggplant
- 3 seaweed sheets
- 2 tablespoons of water
- 2 tablespoons powdered sugar
- 4 tablespoons of rice vinegar
- wasabi-sauce

PREPARATION

1. Cook the sushi rice for 15-20 minutes in a pressure cooker.
2. Meanwhile, prepare your work surface by spreading aluminium foil and a sheet of seaweed on it.
3. Cut the salmon, the tortilla and the piece of eggplant into strips.
4. In a saucepan, bring the water, sugar and rice vinegar to a boil. Pour this mixture into the cooked rice. Mix gently.
5. Place a thin layer of rice on the seaweed sheet, leaving two centimeters on all sides. Arrange the strips of salmon and aubergine.
6. Moisten the ends with the rest of the vinegar sauce.
7. Roll as tightly as possible and cut into chunks.
8. Repeat the process, varying the ingredients.
9. You can also have small mounds of sushi rice and top with salmon or omelette.
10. All you have to do is enjoy with the wasabi sauce.

Fondant carrots with cumin and wild flowers from Provence

Preparation : 15 mins   **Ready in : 25 min**   **Portions : 1 person**

INGREDIENTS

- 1 bunch carrot tops
- 2 tablespoons olive oil
- 1 teaspoon cumin seeds
- 2 litters of chicken broth
- 1 teaspoon chopped parsley
- 1/2 teaspoon of wild flowers from Provence from Nat et Bio
- Salt of Guarantee
- Ground pepper 3 Kerala peppers

PREPARATION

1. Cut your carrot tops leaving 1 to 2 cm.
2. Peel the carrots, wash them and cut them in half lengthwise and in half width wise.
3. Heat your chicken broth and dip your carrots in it, which you will cook for 10 minutes.
4. Drain them and put them in a saucepan over low heat with the olive oil and cumin.
5. Simmer 15 minutes, stirring occasionally.
6. Serve immediately with a little salt, pepper, parsley and wild flowers from Provence.

Endive Gratin

Preparation : 15 mins   **Ready in: 40 min**   **Portions : 4 people**

INGREDIENTS

PREPARATION

- 12 fine chicories
- 6 large slices of white ham
- grated cheese
- 40g flour
- 40 g butter + a little to butter the molds
- 40 cl of milk
- nutmeg
- Salt pepper

1. Pass the endives quickly under water, remove the damaged leaves, clean them, cut the base by making a small incision to remove most of the "core".
2. Pressure cook them "so that the basket keeps them out of the cooking water", 20 minutes from the whisper of the valve.
3. Remove them and put them to drain in a colander for 1 or 2 hours.
4. Prepare your béchamel:
5. Melt the butter, add the flour all at once, mix well with a wooden spoon, then gradually pour in the milk, thicken, stirring constantly, until thickened. Season with salt and pepper and add a little ground nutmeg.
6. Grease the molds with butter, cut the slices of ham in half lengthwise, roll up a curly endive for half a slice of ham,
7. "I made 3 per person", cover with béchamel, sprinkle with grated cheese and bake in a hot oven at 180° for 20 minutes.
8. The top should be golden.

Tagine with Moroccan prunes

Preparation : 45 mins **Ready in: 45 mins** **Portions : 4 people**

INGREDIENTS

- 1 kg leg of lamb
- 500g prunes
- 100 g blanched almonds
- 1 finely chopped onion
- 1 cinnamon stick
- 1 teaspoon ground cinnamon
- 2 tablespoons orange blossom water
- 1 tablespoon of honey
- Olive oil
- Salt, pepper, ginger

PREPARATION

1. In a pressure cooker put the lamb, onion, olive oil, salt, pepper, ginger and cinnamon stick.
2. Simmer over low heat for 5 minutes, stirring occasionally.
3. Cover with water and cook covered for 40 minutes.
4. Add the cinnamon powder and dissolve the honey in the sauce.
5. Wash the prunes and cook them with the meat for ten minutes. Add a little water if necessary.
6. Pour in the orange blossom water and let the sauce reduce. 15 minutes before serving, brown the almonds in the hot oil.

Wheat/Bly with vegetables

Preparation : 30 mins   *Ready in: 15 min*   *Portions : 4 people*

INGREDIENTS	PREPARATION

- 1 cup 1/2 wheat
- 1 large carrot
- 2 zucchinis
- 1 onion
- Thyme

1. Meanwhile, brown the onions, carrots and zucchini in a pan until they take on a nice colour Season with thyme and salt/pepper.
2. Bring it all together.

With Catalan tuna

INGREDIENTS

- 1 large red beet
- 1 can of Catalan tuna
- 1 shallot
- Parsley
- 5 pepper berries

PREPARATION

1. Cook the beets in a pressure cooker, then grate them with a large-hole mandolin.
2. Chop the shallot and a few parsley flakes.
3. Mix everything with the tuna and its sauce. Season with pepper.
4. For this salad, I always grate the beets instead of dicing or slicing them because I think the flavour is better.

Spinach/lentil velouté with curry

Preparation : 15 mins   **Ready in : 30 min**   **Portions : 2 people**

INGREDIENTS

- 1 shallot
- 1 stock cube
- 1 teaspoon olive oil
- 1 teaspoon of curry
- 200g fresh spinach
- 50g raw green lentils
- Pepper (no salt)
- 5cl of 15% cream

PREPARATION

1. Fry the chopped shallot (or alternatively the onion) in olive oil and add the curry. Mix for a few minutes and add the spinach leaves and lentils. To mix together.
2. Add 800 ml of water and the cube (for my part I use the pots).
3. If using a pressure cooker, cook for 15 minutes, otherwise 30 minutes over low heat in a saucepan. Blend in a blender or immersion blender.
4. Before serving, add the cream and cook over low heat for ten minutes.
5. The colour is not necessarily pretty, but it gives a delicious and very comforting soup!

Motorola-style cassoulet

Preparation : 30 mins   **Ready in : 1 hr 30 min**   **Servings : 4 people**

INGREDIENTS

PREPARATION

- 300 g dried beans in ingot
- 4 smoked sausages
- 300g smoked pork belly
- 1 garlic sausage
- 1/2 can of tomato pulp
- 2 cases of tomato puree
- 1 onion
- 3 cloves of garlic
- 1 bouquet garni bay thyme
- Pork fat
- Salt pepper

1. The day before, soak the ingots for 12 hours.
2. The next day, rinse the beans, cook them in 1/2 water for 20 minutes in a pressure cooker.
3. In a Dutch oven, put the butter, the peeled onion, the garlic cloves and the chopped ones.
4. Cut the duck breast into 4 pieces, the sausage into thick slices.
5. Brown the onion, the minced garlic in the butter, add the meat except the sausage.
6. Sauté them, stirring for 10 minutes.
7. Add the tin of tomatoes, the tomato purée, the bouquet garni, salt and pepper.
8. Put the ingot, liter of water stirs well.
9. Cook over low heat for 1 hour, watching the slices of chorizo.
10. And simmer for 30 minutes.

Lentil velouté with surimi

Preparation : 15 mins   **Ready in : 15 min**   **Portions : 4 people**

INGREDIENTS

- 1 small yellow onion olive oil
- 1 liter of vegetable broth
- 250 g coral lentils
- 100 g grated seafood surimi
- 10 cl of milk 40 cl of liquid cream
- 1 can of salmon roe
- 4 carrots

PREPARATION

1. Peel and chop the onion, brown it in the pressure cooker with the oil. When it begins to brown, add the vegetable broth then the lentils. Close the pressure cooker and cook for 15 minutes from the opening of the valve.
2. When the lentils are cooked, add the milk, 50 g of grated shellfish and blend with an immersion blender.
3. Pass the soup through a sieve so that there are no more lumps. Pour the velouté into bowls, spin the pepper mill and decorate with the rest of the surimi after chopping it.
4. Cook the 50g of coral lentils in 30cl of water and set aside.
5. Peel the carrots and cut them into small cubes. Cook them in a liter of boiling salted water for about ten minutes. Drain the carrots and mix them with the rest of the grated surimi and the 50 g of cooked red lentils.
6. Whip the cream and add the salmon eggs.
7. Place a tablespoon of surimi/carrots/lentils in the centre of a deep plate.
8. Place a quenelle of egg whipped cream on top and pour the velouté.

Red cabbage & strainers

Preparation : 30 mins   **Ready in : 1 hr 10 min**   **Servings : 6 people**

INGREDIENTS	PREPARATION

- 1 large red cabbage
- 1 bay leaf
- 15cl of red wine
- 10cl of water
- 5cl of wine vinegar
- 100 g of smoked bacon
- 2 apples
- Salt pepper
- 50 gr of butter + a little to brown the strainers
- 6 crunches

1. Discard the first leaves of the cabbage, cut it into thin strips and wash it. Boil a large quantity of water and blanch the cabbage for ten minutes. Then drain it.
2. In the pressure cooker, melt the butter, put half the cabbage, the diced apples and the bacon bits, then the rest of the cabbage, the bay leaf, salt, pepper, pour in the water, wine, vinegar.
3. In a very hot frying pan, brown the strainers, when they have taken on a nice colour, place them on the cabbage.
4. Close the pan, when the valve whispers, put on low heat and cook for about thirty minutes.
5. If you do not have a pressure cooker, count from 1h to 1h30 in normal cooking.

Pan - fried vegetables with watercress

Preparation : 15 mins   **Ready in: 08 min**   **Portions : 4 people**

INGREDIENTS

- 600 g of poultry (chicken, turkey, etc.)
- 250g carrots
- 3 stalks of celery
- 250g green beans
- 50 cl of chicken broth
- 100 g watercress
- 90g cottage cheese
- Salt pepper
- Tarragon

PREPARATION

1. Season the chicken breasts, peel the carrots and celery.
2. Cut them into thin juliennes and wash the green beans (remove the ends if not already done).
3. -Reserve a little watercress (a handful) and place the rest in the "basket" of the pressure cooker. Arrange the chicken breasts on top, as well as the vegetables.
4. Pour water into the pressure cooker and cook for 7/8 minutes.
5. Meanwhile, bring the chicken broth to a boil, add the handful of watercress and mix. Let this mixture reduce. Add the cream cheese and mix again. Then, either you mix this sauce with the dish, or you reserve it and serve it at the same time as the dish, it's up to you. Add the tarragon and you're done!

Prunes in red dress

Preparation : 30 mins   *Ready in : 5 to 10 min*   *Servings : 6 people*

INGREDIENTS

- 500g Agen prunes
- 500g strawberries
- 4 tablespoons of Grand-Marnier or Cointreau
- For the syrup:
- 150 g) sugar
- 1 glass of water
- Juice of 2 medium oranges

PREPARATION

1. Steam the plums by placing them in a colander in a large saucepan containing a few inches of boiling water, or by placing the colander in a pressure cooker containing the same amount of water. 15 minutes in a covered regular saucepan, 5 minutes in a pressure cooker.
2. Meanwhile, mix the syrup ingredients and cook for 5 minutes after boiling. Let cool.
3. Peel the strawberries and cut them in half if they are large.
4. Arrange the prunes and strawberries in individual cups.
5. Add Grand-Marnier or Cointreau to the cooled syrup. Pour over the fruit bowls and leave to macerate in the fridge for a few hours before serving.

Quick and Delicious Mussels in Tomato Sauce

Preparation : 45 mins   **Ready in : 20 mins**   **Portions : 4 people**

INGREDIENTS

- 2 kg of mussels
- 1 can diced tomatoes
- 2 cloves garlic
- 1 onion
- Parsley

PREPARATION

1. In a saucepan with a little oil, brown the onion cut into small pieces, let it brown very slightly.
2. Add the chopped tomatoes, bay leaf, parsley and whole garlic (don't forget to remove the germ.
3. Check the seasoning and simmer for about 20 minutes over very low heat.
4. Meanwhile, clean your muscles.
5. For mussel cleaning, sort out chipped or damaged mussels. Discard the opened mussels.
6. Molds should be tightly closed and stored in a cool place where they can be opened.
7. Rinse the mussels and remove the beard with a knife.
8. Pressure cooker cooking:
9. Put the mussels in the pressure cooker 5 minutes before eating them.
10. Increase the pressure in the pressure cooker and turn off the heat, leave 5 minutes without opening.
11. Dutch oven cooking:
12. Add the mussels to the pot and cook until they open,
13. Stir once or twice for even cooking.
14. Just before serving, drain the water from the mussels,
15. Reserve a large glass of water which is poured over the tomato sauce if it is too thick, and immediately afterwards over the mussels.

Swiss chard gratin

Preparation : 30 mins   Ready in : 40 min   Portions : 4 people

INGREDIENTS

PREPARATION

- 700g chard
- 40cl of milk
- A little flour
- 20g butter
- 1 can of mustard
- Salt pepper

1. Peel the chard, cut them into small pieces, wash them and cook them in a pressure cooker for 10 to 15 minutes.
2. Prepare the béchamel: melt the butter add a little flour, milk, mustard, salt and pepper while mixing, let thicken.
3. Arrange the chard in a gratin dish, add the béchamel sauce and the grated cheese, bake for about 25 minutes. 6 (180°C).

Homemade mashed potatoes

Preparation : 15 mins   **Ready in : 15 min**   **Portions : 3 people**

INGREDIENTS

- 20 small potatoes
- 15 cl of milk
- 5 cl of cream
- Salt pepper
- Nutmeg

PREPARATION

1. Peel and wash the potatoes in water.
2. Cook them in the pressure cooker for about 15 minutes. When potatoes are cooked in a potato masher. Add milk, cream, salt, pepper, mix. Then add the nutmeg, mix.

Endive gratin with ricotta

Preparation : 15 mins   Ready in : 15 min   Portions : 4 people

INGREDIENTS	PREPARATION

INGREDIENTS

- 10 chicories
- 10 slices of ham (preferably smoked)
- 1 can of ricotta
- 40g butter
- 40g flour
- 50 cl of milk
- Salt, pepper, nutmeg

PREPARATION

1. The day before, cook the endives in a pressure cooker (it is advisable to do this the day before because the endives give off a lot of water). Prepare the béchamel sauce: melt the butter, add the flour, beat with a whisk and gradually add the milk, salt and pepper, add the nutmeg and wait for the sauce to thicken.
2. (You can add grated cheese if you like).
3. Spread the ricotta over the slices of ham,
4. Place an endive in the centre of each slice.
5. And roll the ham around the escarole.
6. Place in a baking dish and add the bechamel sauce. Bake for 15 minutes in a hot oven.

Beef cheek stew

Preparation : 1 hour 30 minutes   Ready in : 1 hr 50 min   Servings : 8 people

INGREDIENTS

- 2 kg beef cheek
- 200 g pieces of plain bacon
- 1kg of carrots
- 1 kg of onions
- 3 cloves of garlic
- 1 liter of red wine
- Laurel
- Olive oil
- Thyme
- Salt

PREPARATION

1. Soak the meat for 1 hour in the wine with the sliced onions, the bay leaf and the thin. Drain the meat. In a pressure cooker, brown the bacon, the onions, the beef cheek in the olive oil.

2. Add the carrots cut in sections, the whole garlic in shirt. Cover the volume of meat with the wine. Leave to cook for 60 minutes.

3. Stop cooking, leave to cool for 30 minutes, then resume cooking uncovered over very low heat for 20 minutes. Enjoy the double with white rice.

Duo of cabbage with chestnuts

Preparation : 15 mins **Ready in : 30 min** **Portions : 6 people**

INGREDIENTS

- 1 small red cabbage
- 1 small white cabbage
- 800g onions
- 1 good piece of bacon
- 1 kg of chestnuts
- Salt
- Pepper
- Thyme
- 1 bay leaf
- Oil

PREPARATION

1. Cut each cabbage, separately, into quarters and then into strips. Wash the red and white cabbage separately.
2. Blanch each cabbage separately for 5 minutes.
3. Cut the bacon into thick slices. In a non-stick pan, brown it quickly. To book.
4. Peel the onions and cut them finely. Heat the oil in a pressure cooker and brown them. Add cabbage, bacon, lots of thyme, bay leaf, salt and pepper. Mix well.
5. Bake 20 mins.
6. Add the chestnuts and cook for another 10 minutes without pressure.

Carrot & Pumpkin Velouté

Preparation : 15 mins   *Servings : 8 people*

INGREDIENTS

- 1 kg of carrots
- 1 kg of pumpkin pulp
- 1 stalk of celery in pieces
- 1 large onion, chopped
- 1 crushed garlic clove
- 1 handful of trumpets of death (mushrooms)
- 2 nails

PREPARATION

1. Put all the ingredients in a pressure cooker. Add water to the height of the vegetables and pressurize.
2. As soon as it is under pressure, lower the heat and count 15 minutes.
3. Mix everything together and enjoy with or without grated cheese.

Oxtail terrine

Preparation : 15 mins   **Ready in : 1 hr**   **Servings : 6 people**

INGREDIENTS

- 1 good oxtail in sections
- 1 bouquet garni (thyme, bay leaf, parsley)
- 1 onion
- 1 carrot
- 6 nails
- 1 handful of coarse salt

For the tomato coulis:

- 6 fresh tomatoes (or 1 can of crushed tomatoes)
- 1/2 red wine
- 2 cloves garlic, minced (or 2 teaspoons frozen garlic
- 300g mushrooms

PREPARATION

1. Place the oxtail sections in a pressure cooker. Add the bouquet garni, the onion studded with 6 cloves, the carrot and the coarse salt. Cover with cold water, add the red wine to the level and cook for 60 minutes from the turn of the valve.
2. When the meat is cooked, drain it and separate it carefully (being careful not to leave any leftover bones). Filter 50 cl of broth, put it in a saucepan and reduce it by half (about 20 minutes over medium heat).
3. Meanwhile, prepare the tomato coulis. If the tomatoes are fresh, simply cut them into cubes, taking care to remove the stringy part at the base.
4. Mix all the ingredients, salt and pepper to taste.
5. When the broth has reduced by half, mix it with the meat and put the porcini mushrooms in a pan with a knob of butter and put in a terrine. Then let it sit in the refrigerator for at least 5-6 hours.

Grilled veal cutlets with vegetables

Preparation : 15 mins   **Ready in : mins**   **Servings : 2 people**

INGREDIENTS

- 2 veal cutlets
- Salt
- Pepper
- 1 clove garlic very finely chopped
- 2 zucchinis
- Broccoli florets
- 2 tablespoons olive oil
- 1 lemon

PREPARATION

1. Remove the green leaves, the brown parts around the bouquet. Pour the vinegar into a container. Add the broccoli florets to eliminate insects and slugs. Wash each bouquet under running water and place them in a colander to drain. Cut the courgettes into pieces.

2. Put the container for vegetables, it is perforated with holes. Review your instructions carefully. You can of course use your pressure cooker. Pepper the chops and grill for 3 minutes on each side, then salt, add the lemon juice to the chops. Arrange the chops on warm plates.

3. Serve with steamed vegetables and a drizzle of olive oil.

Fried rice my way

Preparation : 30 mins   *Servings : 4 people*

INGREDIENTS	PREPARATION

- 200g shelled prawns
- 150 g bean sprouts
- 300g rice
- 4 beaten eggs in tortilla
- 1 green pepper
- Yellow and red cubed
- 150 g of bacon
- 100g ham
- 1 carrot cut into strips
- Olive oil
- Salt
- Pepper
- Siave and nuoc Nam sauce
- Then a little sherry vinegar.

1. Fry the prawns in a pan with olive oil, then the bacon bits and then the eggs in an omelette. Cut the eggs into strips as well as the carrots, peppers into cubes or strips.
2. Cook the rice in a pressure cooker, then add it to all the mixtures and season with salt, pepper, sieve, nuoc Nam sauce and then sherry vinegar.

Eggs with asparagus

Preparation : 15 mins   **Ready in : 11 min**   **Portions : 6 people**

INGREDIENTS

- 2 kg of asparagus
- 10 eggs
- 30g butter
- 10 cl fresh cream
- Salt
- Pepper

PREPARATION

1. Order the asparagus. Cook them in a pressure cooker basket, cook 5 minutes from the bottom of the pan.
2. Melt 15 g of butter in a frying pan and brown the asparagus for a few minutes.
3. Crack the eggs into a bowl, season with salt and pepper. Pierce the yolks but do not beat.
4. Melt the rest of the butter in a saucepan, pour in the eggs, stirring constantly for 10 minutes. Add the fresh cream and continue cooking for 1 minute, stirring.
5. Serve eggs and garnish with asparagus.

Pumpkin soup, liquid chicory

Preparation : 15 mins   **Ready in: 12 min**   **Portions : 4 people**

INGREDIENTS

- 1 kg pumpkin NET (after peeling),
- 1 liter of filtered water,
- 2 cubes of organic chicken broth AB,
- 1 tablespoon of sunflower oil,
- 1 C. coffee of Leroux liquid chicory (optional but delicate pairing with the pumpkin.

PREPARATION

1. Fry the chopped pumpkin for 2 to 3 minutes in hot oil, stirring constantly.
2. Add boiling water (think kettle), chicory and cubes (think kettle).
3. Cook for 12 minutes in the pressure cooker from the whistle.
4. Blend with an immersion blender.

Red plums in syrup

Preparation : 15 mins **Ready in: 25 min** **Portions : 1 person**

INGREDIENTS

PREPARATION

- For 1 kg of plums add ½ liter of water and 250 g of sugar

1. Bring the water and sugar to a boil and let cool.
2. Put the plums in the jars and pour the cold sugar syrup up to a maximum of 2 cm from the top edge of the jar.
3. Put the jars in your pressure cooker, Dutch oven or sterilizer. Separate them with paper towels so they don't collide. Pour cold water up to 1 cm above the jars. Boil water for 25 minutes and let cool.
4. When everything is cold, take out the jars, clean them and store them away from light.
5. In order to be able to store plums for this winter without cluttering up my freezer, I decided to put some in a jar.
6. I advise you to pack well in the jar (without crushing the plums)

Pumpkin and chestnut velouté

INGREDIENTS

- 1kg 500 about pumpkin
- 500 g of chestnuts
- A small jar of fresh cream (10cl)
- Butter 50g
- Salt
- Flora line

PREPARATION

1. Put the chestnuts to cook in a saucepan with salted water, during this time peel and wash the pumpkin and cut it into large cubes, once the chestnuts are cooked peel them (I prepared my chestnuts the day before) in a pressure cooker put the pumpkin and chestnuts are covered with boiling water and salt and cooked 15m from the whistle.

2. Once cooked, mix everything together, add the butter, the saucepan of fresh cream, mix well and put back on the heat, add a few tablespoons of flora line, stirring constantly to thicken your velouté, cook for a few minutes, adjust the salt to your taste and that's it.

3. This autumn velouté is a gourmet delight with the association of pumpkin and chestnuts and very easy to prepare.

4. Sometimes the simple things are the best.

Green beans with chicken meatballs

Preparation : 30 mins   **Ready in : 5 to 10 min**   **Servings : 4 people**

INGREDIENTS

- 4 chicken burgers
- 1 onion
- 3 tablespoons of olive oil
- 3 carrots
- 3 potatoes
- 400g frozen green beans
- 1/2 chicken stock cube
- 300ml water
- 3 tablespoons of flour
- 1 Bonduelle box to fry
- Salt pepper
- 1 egg yolk
- Parsley

PREPARATION

1. Start mixing the minced meat, but not too much, with an egg yolk, pepper and a little salt, you can add parsley, which I forgot, spread the palms of your hands with oil, shape them into meatballs then roll them in the flour.

2. Heat the olive oil in the frying pan over high heat, sauté the minced onion, the carrots after having cut them into small cubes, then the chicken meatballs.... Sauté for 5 minutes then lower the heat... Pepper.... Crumble the half-cube of chicken broth, mix lightly with the frozen green beans, add the potatoes... Sprinkle with a good glass of water.

3. Continue cooking in the pressure cooker for 6 minutes from the end of cooking, pour the contents of the can of mushrooms into the tomato and cook again over low heat for 3 minutes.

4. Serve immediately hot.

Leeks with ham gratin

Preparation : 15 mins   **Ready in : 25 min**   **Portions : 2 people**

INGREDIENTS

- 2 leeks
- 2 slices of defatted white ham
- 1 briquette of light soy cream
- 50 g of escamorzo
- 1 clove garlic, degermed
- Salt pepper

PREPARATION

1. Peel, wash the leeks carefully. Cut the green and save it for a good soup.
2. Cut the egg white into 5 parts (4 equivalents, the rest will be mixed).
3. Cook the leeks in the pressure cooker in the steamer basket for 15 minutes.
4. Preheat the oven to 180° with convection.
5. Drain. Press a little to evacuate the most liquid of the vegetation. To book.
6. Cut the slices of ham in 2.
7. Surround the slices of white leek with a 1/2 slice of ham each. Reserve the last for the topping sauce.
8. Place the rolls in a baking dish.
9. Mix the reserved part with the degermed garlic clove, the scamorza.
10. Add the soy cream. Salt, pepper, mix.
11. Pour over ham rolls.
12. Bake for the first 20 minutes then finish cooking by grilling for 5 minutes to brown.

Salad From the Sea

Preparation : 15 mins   *Ready in: 40 min*   *Portions : 2 people*

INGREDIENTS

- 500g octopus tentacles
- 3 tomatoes
- 100 g of cooked wheat semolina
- 1 stalk of celery
- 1 sprig of garlic
- 1 lemon
- Parsley
- 1 tablespoon olive oil
- Salt pepper

PREPARATION

1. Wash the tentacles and remove the skin.
2. Put in the pressure cooker, cover with water, and cook 35/40 minutes from the murmur.
3. Drain and run under cold water, removing any skin residue.
4. Cut the octopus into small strips. To book.
5. Clean and cut the tomatoes and celery into small cubes.
6. Finely chop the garlic.
7. In a salad bowl, combine the cut octopus, the tomatoes, the celery, the garlic and the cooked wheat groats.
8. Add olive oil, lemon juice, chopped parsley.
9. Salt, pepper, mix.
10. Wrap and refrigerate for at least an hour before serving.

Charcuterie Cold Pork Roast

INGREDIENTS

- 1 pork roast of 1 kg
- 15g of butter
- 1 tablespoon oil
- Salt pepper
- 1 onion
- 1 clove
- Bouquet garni

PREPARATION

1. In the pressure cooker, bring 1 1/2 litters of water to a boil with salt, pepper, onion studded with cloves, bouquet garni.
2. Brown the roast well on all sides in a skillet with the butter and oil.
3. When the meat is nicely browned, plunge it into the boiling broth of the pressure cooker. Close this. Simmer 30 minutes from pressure setting.
4. Drain the roast as soon as it is cooked. Let cool completely, overnight, if possible, before slicing.
5. Present the roasted sausage with mustard, pickles, tomatoes, mayonnaise, salad and olives.

Lamb shank, beans

Preparation : 15 mins   *Ready in : 20 mins*   *Portions : 4 people*

INGREDIENTS

- Leg of lamb 600g
- 6 potatoes
- 1 can of paprika
- 1 chopped onion
- 3 cloves of garlic
- 4 sprigs of thyme
- 1 bay leaf
- 300 g flageolet beans
- flower of salt
- Ground pepper
- Homemade tomato sauce if possible if not purchased.

PREPARATION

1. The day before, soak the beans in cold water. The next day, sauté the peeled and chopped onion, as well as the garlic.
2. Brown mouse on all sides book.
3. Put the beans in the pressure cooker, along with the tomato sauce, onion, garlic, salt, pepper, thyme, bay leaf, 3 pots of water, and the mouse and potatoes.
4. Bake for 20 minutes.

Single entry steamed courgettes

Preparation : 15 mins   **Ready in : 5 to 10 min**   **Servings : 3 people**

INGREDIENTS

- 1 good zucchini
- 1 case of strong mustard
- 2 cases of olive oil
- 1 case of cider vinegar
- Salt pepper
- Garlic
- Parsley

PREPARATION

1. Wash the zucchini cut into 5 cm sections
2. Put them in the steamer basket of the pressure cooker and add a glass of water to the bottom with 1/2 a glass of coarse salt, cook for 10 minutes.
3. Once cooked, take them out and let them cool.
4. Arrange them on a plate.
5. Prepare the dressing.
6. Peel the garlic, remove the germ, pass it through a chopper.
7. Wash the parsley, chop it.
8. Sprinkle all the zucchini, drizzle with vinaigrette and enjoy

Mediterranean cuttlefish

Preparation : 15 mins   Ready in : 4 hrs 15 mins   Portions : 4 people

INGREDIENTS

- 1 kg of cuttlefish
- 1 kg of tomatoes
- 500g of mushrooms
- chicken stock cube
- 1 glass of white wine
- 1 onion
- 2 thyme leaves
- Fresh cream

PREPARATION

1. Cook the cuttlefish in the pressure cooker (about 1/4 hour depending on the size).
2. Meanwhile brown the onion, mushrooms.
3. Add the tomatoes and cook over low heat for 10 minutes.
4. Add the chicken broth with a little water and the white wine + thyme.
5. Once the tomatoes are cooked, add the cuttlefish and sprinkle with a little cream.
6. Simmer for about 5 more minutes.

Stuffed peppers

Preparation : 45 mins   **Ready in : 20 mins**   **Portions : 4 people**

INGREDIENTS

- 4 large sweet peppers (wider than long)
- 1 large can of tomato sauce
- 1 chopped onion
- 2 knobs of butter
- 1 glass of rice
- 1 glass of water
- 300g minced meat
- 1 egg 1 clove garlic thyme, leaves removed
- 1 C. paprika
- Salt pepper

PREPARATION

1. In the pressure cooker, brown the onion with a knob of butter. Add rice, water, salt and pepper. Close the pressure cooker. Cook for exactly 5 minutes over low heat. Meanwhile, brown the minced meat in a pan with a knob of butter.

2. Remove from the pressure cooker, the rice still firm. Mix with the browned meat, lightly beaten egg, minced garlic, thyme leaves, paprika, salt and pepper. Wash the peppers and cut them in each, tail side. Empty them of their seeds without piercing them. Place the stuffing inside and place them upright, side by side in the pressure cooker.

3. Cover them with their little lid to prevent the filling from coming out. Pour the tomato sauce over the peppers. Close the pressure cooker and cook over low heat for 15 minutes. You can serve them as a starter, hot or cold.

Fish sauerkraut

Preparation : 45 mins   **Ready in : 40 min**   **Portions : 8 people**

INGREDIENTS

- 4 salmon fillets of 200g each
- 8 monkfish medallions
- 600g cod
- About 1.7 kg of sauerkraut
- 1/2 bunch of dill
- 4 shallots
- 2 chopped onions
- 15g of butter
- 2 sachets of court broth
- 35 cl of dry white wine
- 20 cl of liquid cream
- 1 tablespoon of juniper berries
- 2 tablespoons olive oil
- 1 teaspoon cornstarch
- Salt
- Pepper

PREPARATION

1. In a pressure cooker, melt the onions in the oil without browning them. Add the sauerkraut, juniper berries, 20 cl of water and 20 cl of white wine. Close tightly and cook for 40 minutes.

2. Meanwhile, chop the dill. Peel and chop the shallots, put them in a saucepan with the butter and let them melt for 5 minutes. Pour the rest of the wine and cook over low heat for another 5 minutes. Add the cream and cornstarch dissolved in a tablespoon of water. Salt pepper. Cook for 3 minutes over medium heat, stirring. Add the dill. Keep warm in a bain-marie.

3. Cut the salmon fillets in 2 and the cod in equal parts. Dilute the cutting broth in a pan of water. Add the salmon, monkfish and cod. Bring to a boil and simmer for 5 to 7 minutes.

4. Spread the sauerkraut on a large warm plate. Garnish with the drained fish pieces. Present the sauce in a sauce boat.

Slice of quinoa Macedonia roast pork

INGREDIENTS	PREPARATION
• 8 slices of roast • 800 g of mixed salad • 200g organic quinoa • Extra light fresh cream (4%) a briquette • Salt with spices • Sichuan pepper with cardamom and coriander seeds.	1. Cook the salad for 5 minutes (pressure cooker). 2. Put the slices of roast in a pan and cook for ten minutes. Set aside, put the salad in its place with the fresh cream. 3. Rinse the quinoa with plenty of water, cook it as indicated on its packaging. 4. Add to the salad, mix, reheat with the slices of meat, adjust the seasoning if necessary.

Salmon with coconut milk spinach shallot garlic and fresh ginger

---

Preparation : 15 mins   *Ready in: 15 min*   *Portions : 8 people*

INGREDIENTS

PREPARATION

- Fresh wild salmon 2 pieces of 150gr each
- 2 large shallots
- Garlic 2 beautiful degermed
- Fresh ginger 3cm
- Coconut milk 1/2 briquettes
- Special seaweed fish salt
- Ground pepper
- Frozen spinach 500 gr

1. Cut the skin off the salmon (to prevent it from curling up). Peel the shallots, garlic, ginger (with my tip).
2. Chop the shallots, garlic, grate the ginger. Brown the shallots well, add the garlic, grated ginger, mix and set aside.
3. Put the salmon back on the skin side that you will have salted and seasoned on the flesh side.
4. Add shallots, garlic, ginger and coconut milk and simmer covered for 5 minutes.
5. Meanwhile, steam the frozen spinach for 10 minutes (pressure cooker).
6. Once cooked add them to the pan, before removing the salmon, set aside, mix your spinach, salt and pepper, add the salmon, reheat for 5 minutes, serve and enjoy.

Saddle of lamb roasted Spanish beans roasted potato

Preparation : 15 mins   Ready in : 2 h 05 min   Portions : 3 people

INGREDIENTS	PREPARATION

INGREDIENTS

- Saddle of lamb 450gr
- Potatoes 3 medium
- Shallots 3 garlic cloves 4 peeled
- Green beans 300 gr
- Parsley
- spring onion
- Thyme
- garden sage
- Salt with spices and Espelette pepper
- Sichuan pepper
- Coriander seeds
- Cardamom seeds

PREPARATION

1. Prick the rack of lamb with the peeled and degermed garlic.
2. Brown the saddle well, especially on the fat and crispy side, set aside. Fry the peeled and diced shallots in a little olive oil.
3. We also add the peeled and chopped potatoes. Salt and pepper.
4. Mix, add the seasoned loin to the pan (on the stone, if possible, much better cooking), cover and cook for 1/2 hour, stirring occasionally.
5. Meanwhile, steam the beans for 5 minutes (pressure cooker).
6. As for cooking the cooked loin, take it out and put the beans in its place, personally I added half a pot of crushed tomato from the garden that I had left.
7. Add the remaining garlic, sage, parsley, thyme, chopped chives, mix, heat very gently.
8. Cut the saddle into thin slices. Serve with vegetables and good

Baking potatoes

Preparation : 30 mins   *Ready in: 12 min*   *Portions : 4 people*

INGREDIENTS

PREPARATION

- 1 kg potato
- 3 or 4 onions
- 30g bouquet garni butter
- 2 cloves garlic
- Salt and pepper
- 1 or 2 glasses of boiling water
- 1 tablet of concentrated stock

1. Peel and cut the onions into rings. Brown them lightly in a pan with 25g of butter.
2. Meanwhile, peel and cut the potatoes into slices but not too thin. Then wash them (the cooking will be better) and clean them.
3. Butter the inside of the pressure cooker and place half the potato slices on it.
4. Spread the golden onions on top, then the leftover potatoes, bouquet garni and garlic cloves. Salt and pepper.
5. Pour into the pressure cooker 1 or 2 glasses of water, in which you will have dissolved the broth concentrate. Close the pressure cooker and cook for 12 minutes under pressure.
6. Remove the bouquet garni before serving the bakery bakers.

Veal liver with carrots and prunes

Preparation : 30 mins   **Ready in : 23 min**   **Portions : 4 people**

INGREDIENTS	PREPARATION

INGREDIENTS

- 4 slices of beef liver
- 100 g smoked bacon
- 1kg of carrots
- 4 small onions
- 250g Agen prunes
- 60g butter
- 1 glass of dry white wine
- 2 tablespoons of flour
- 2 tablespoons chopped parsley
- Salt and pepper

PREPARATION

1. The day before, put the prunes on a plate, sprinkle with white wine and leave to macerate overnight.
2. The same day, peel and wash the carrots, then cut them into slices 1 cm thick.
3. Peel and chop the small onions.
4. Heat 30 g of butter in a pressure cooker over low heat and sauté the bacon bits and onion for 5 minutes.
5. Add the carrot slices, moisten with the prune maceration wine and cook for 10 minutes under pressure. Salt, add the prunes and continue cooking for 5 minutes.
6. Flour the slices of liver and brown them with the remaining butter in a skillet over high heat, 3 minutes on each side. Salt and pepper.
7. Arrange the slices of liver on a dish, surround with carrots and prunes, sprinkle with parsley and serve immediately.

Parmentier 3 florets (broccoli, cauliflower, Romanesco cabbage). With 3 fish (salmon, monkfish, cod)

Preparation : 30 mins   *Ready in: 20 mins*   *Portions : 6 people*

INGREDIENTS

- 1Kg 3 flowers
- 750 Gr 3 fish (your choice)
- 2 medium potatoes
- A little light cream or not
- Grated
- Salt pepper
- Nutmeg
- 2 shallots
- 2cm fresh ginger
- Herbs (I choose dill, parsley, sage)

PREPARATION

1. the 3 florets for 10 mins in the potato (pressure cooker), do the same with the 3 fish (your choice) for 15 mins.
2. Crush the potato and the bouquets with a fork, add the cream with a grater, mix gently with a hand whisk so that it is not too homogeneous.
3. Chop the herbs (optional), mix the shallots with the fresh ginger.
4. Spread the 3 bouquets in the bottom of a small cheesecake mould, alternate with the 3 fish, then the 3 bouquets.
5. Do the same with the other 5 molds.
6. Bake at 150c for 20 mins.

Velouté of broccoli with cheese (lightened fresh square

Preparation : 15 mins   **Ready in : 15 min**   **Portions : 4 people**

INGREDIENTS	PREPARATION

- 1 kg frozen broccoli
- 4 fresh squares 0% (cheese)
- 1 liter of water
- 2 defatted chicken stock cubes
- Pepper.

1. Steam the broccoli for 15 minutes (pressure cooker).
2. Put them in the blender, add the fresh squares, remix, taste.
3. Adjust the seasoning if necessary

Colombo Pork

INGREDIENTS

PREPARATION

- 2 pork shanks
- 1 or 2 eggplants
- 2 onions
- 2 bay leaves
- 2 cloves garlic
- 1 lime
- 1 West Indian pepper
- 2 pounds of potatoes
- 4 tablespoons powdered Colombo
- 2 tablespoons chopped parsley
- Oil
- Salt

1. The day before, marinate the shanks (cut into large pieces and degreased) adding the skin, with the lemon juice, the puff pastry onions, the garlic cut into small pieces, the salt and cover with water.

2. The next day, drain the meat and all the marinade ingredients. Dry them with a cloth then brown them in a pressure cooker with oil.

3. Add the peeled and chopped eggplant. When everything is nicely browned, add the Colombo powder and chopped parsley, then pour in the marinade water and salt. Let cook for about 1/2 hour.

4. Add the potatoes cut into large chunks and a West Indian pepper on top so as not to sting it... And cook again for about 20 minutes.

5. Then remove the lid and let the sauce reduce over low heat for about 1/2 hour.

6. Serve with white rice (you can add lemon avocado wedges on the edge of the plate).

Rosemary Roast Beef

Preparation : 15 mins   **Ready in : 05 min**   **Portions : 4 people**

INGREDIENTS

- 800 g of sirloin
- 1 sprig of rosemary
- 25g butter
- 2 tablespoons olive oil
- 1/2 glass of red wine
- Salt

PREPARATION

1. Heat the oil in the pressure cooker, then tie the meat and brown it on both sides with the rosemary. Salt and pour the red wine and close. 5 min of cooking from the beep of the valve.
2. Turn off the heat and let the meat rest for a few minutes in the closed pressure cooker, then release the steam.
3. Open and add the butter. Serve the sliced roast beef topped with a drained cooking broth with scpezzeleu or potatoes.

Venetian green beans

Preparation : 15 mins   Ready in : 1 hr   Servings : 4 people

INGREDIENTS

- 1 kg of green beans
- 60 grams of butter
- 1 onion
- 500 grams of firm tomatoes
- 1 clove of garlic
- 1 bunch of herbs
- 2 pinches of oregano (or dried marjoram).
- Salt
- Pepper
- Parsley

PREPARATION

1. Peel the green beans (break off the ends, remove the strings).
2. Wash them.
3. Drain them.
4. Melt 50 grams of butter in a saucepan.
5. Add the chopped onion to it.
6. Add the peeled, seeded and crushed tomatoes, then the green beans, garlic clove, bouquet garni, oregano, salt and pepper.
7. Covers very well.
8. Cook for 1h30 over very low heat (about 35 minutes in a pressure cooker).
9. At the end of this time, remove the bouquet garni.
10. Sprinkle with the remaining butter divided into small hazelnuts and chopped parsley.

Leek sticks

Preparation : 15 mins   Ready in : 5 to 10 min   Servings : 4 people

INGREDIENTS

- 1 kg of leeks
- 1 egg
- 2 tablespoons of flour
- Breadcrumbs
- 1 tablespoon of sunflower oil
- Salt
- Pepper

PREPARATION

1. Cook the leek whites for 8 months in a pressure cooker in salted water.
2. Drain and pat the leeks.
3. Cut sticks 7 to 8 cm long.
4. Coat the leeks in the flour, in the beaten egg with salt and pepper. Go through the breadcrumbs.
5. Heat the oil in a saucepan, brown the leek sticks little by little.
6. Drain on paper towels.
7. Enjoy hot!

Cauliflower salad with parsley

Preparation : 15 mins   **Ready in: 5 to 10 min**   **Servings : 2 people**

INGREDIENTS

- 500g cauliflower
- 1/2 bunch flat-leaf parsley, chopped
- 3 cloves of garlic
- Alcohol vinegar
- Olive oil
- Salt, cumin, paprika

PREPARATION

1. Wash and cut the cauliflower, put it with the whole garlic cloves in a pressure cooker and cook covered for 10 minutes.
2. Crush the garlic in a bowl and add the cauliflower.
3. Add the cumin, salt, paprika, parsley, olive oil and vinegar.
4. Gently mix everything together.

Carrot and parsley salad

Preparation : 15 mins   Ready in : 5 to 10 min   Servings : 6 people

INGREDIENTS

- 1kg of carrots
- 1/2 bunch flat-leaf parsley, chopped
- 2 cloves garlic
- Alcohol vinegar
- Olive oil
- Salt, cumin, paprika

PREPARATION

1. Place whole carrots and garlic cloves in a pressure cooker and cook covered for 10 minutes.
2. Crush the garlic in a bowl and add the quartered carrots.
3. Add the cumin, salt, paprika, parsley, olive oil and vinegar.
4. Gently mix everything together.

Turkey cutlets with cream

Preparation : 15 mins   *Servings : 4 people*

INGREDIENTS

- 600g turkey cutlets
- 40g butter
- 250g mushrooms
- 5dl of wood
- Salt and pepper
- 1 teaspoon sweet mustard
- 2 tablespoons fresh cream

PREPARATION

1. Fry 600 g of turkey cutlets in 40 g of butter.
2. Add 250 g of mushrooms cut into thin strips.
3. Let the water released by the mushrooms evaporate, then add 5 dl of Madeira, salt and pepper.
4. Let it cook for five to six minutes.
5. When ready to serve, remove the turkey cutlets from the pan.
6. Mix the sauce with a teaspoon of sweet mustard and two tablespoons of fresh cream, beat with a sauce mixer.
7. Coat the turkey cutlets with the sauce, serve immediately with steamed potatoes cooked in the pressure cooker.

Mom's Stew

Preparation : 2 hours   Ready in : 2 hrs 15 mins   Portions : 4 people

INGREDIENTS	PREPARATION

INGREDIENTS

- 600 G pork belly 1/2 salt (or shoulder)
- 1 nice onion
- 7 carrots
- 6 large potatoes
- 1/2 green cabbage
- 3 tablespoons of flour
- A good piece of butter 1/2 salt
- 1/2 liter of water
- Pepper
- Thyme
- Laurel

PREPARATION

1. Desalinate the pork for 1 day in cold water or wash it several times by hand under running water
2. Prepare the vegetables:
3. Cut the cabbage into 4, blanch in boiling water, drain and set aside.
4. Peel the carrots and potatoes and cut them into small cubes.
5. Chop the onion (obviously don't forget to peel it first).
6. Put the butter in a large saucepan over high heat, brown, as soon as the butter foams (hazelnut butter) add the flour and cook a little, stirring with a wooden spoon, the mixture should be dark brown.
7. Moisten with cold water and mix with a whisk.
8. Add the meat, the vegetables, everything should be barely covered with water.
9. Pepper, thyme and bay leaf.
10. Do not salt, I adjust at the end of cooking because the meat is often still salty.
11. Cook for 1h30 on medium heat or 45 minutes in a pressure cooker.

Rabbit casserole

Preparation : 45 mins   **Ready in : 45 mins**   **Portions : 4 people**

INGREDIENTS

- 1 Rabbit of about 1,800Kg
- Garlic
- Onion
- 10 beautiful carrots
- Smoked brisket matches
- 2 cans of flour
- Olive oil
- Salt
- Pepper
- Thyme
- Laurel

PREPARATION

1. Cut the rabbit into pieces, reserving the head, liver and heart.
2. Peel and cut the carrots into cubes.
3. Chop the previously peeled onion.
4. Brown the rabbit in hot oil.
5. Set the meat aside.
6. Put the bacon, add the onions, melt them.
7. Put the meat back, mix with the flour, mix vigorously, moisten with cold water.
8. Add head and giblets.
9. Add carrots, spices and herbs (if you want a complete dish, add peeled and cubed potatoes).
10. Cook 40 to 45 minutes or 30 minutes in the pressure cooker.
11. Serve with pasta (unless you added potatoes).

Leek and potato soup

Preparation : 30 mins   *Ready in : 30 min*   *Portions : 6 people*

INGREDIENTS

- 750g leeks
- 750g potatoes
- 40g butter
- 6 sprigs of flat-leaf parsley
- Salt

PREPARATION

1. Split the leeks and rinse them carefully, then drain them and cut them into slices.
2. Peel the potatoes, wash them and cut them into cubes.
3. Heat the butter in a saucepan.
4. Sauté the chopped leeks for 10 minutes over low heat, making sure they brown.
5. Do not colour.
6. Pour 1.5 litters of water (or chicken broth) into the pan.
7. Salt, then add the potatoes.
8. Cover and cook for 20 minutes over low heat.
9. Wash and drain the parsley then chop it.
10. Adjust the seasoning at the end of cooking.
11. Sprinkle with chopped parsley and serve hot.

Red bean minestrone

Preparation : 2 hours   **Ready in : 1 hr 40 min**   **Servings : 4 people**

INGREDIENTS

PREPARATION

- 300g red beans
- 1 onion
- 2 stalks of celery
- 1 carrot
- 1 white leek
- 1 tomato
- 60g butter
- 200 g pasta (large cut macaroni for example)
- Salt
- Ground pepper

1. The night before, soak the kidney beans in cold water.
2. The next day, drain them, put them in 2 litters of cold water without salt and boil for 1h30 with the pan open (or 40 minutes in a pressure cooker).
3. Salt at the end of cooking.
4. Peel the vegetables, then finely chop the onion, finely chop the white leek, cut the celery and the carrot into small pieces, immerse the tomato in boiling water then in cold water and peel it before dice it.
5. Melt the butter in a saucepan and brown the vegetables, adding the diced tomatoes last.
6. Mix well and let brown slightly, salt, pepper.
7. Using a slotted spoon, put the beans with the other vegetables.
8. After 10 minutes of cooking, add the cooking water from the beans.
9. Bring to a boil, add the pasta, boil for 10 minutes and serve.
   ** Can be served with grated cheese.
   **In season, add chopped basil.
   ** Can be served cold.

Printed in Great Britain
by Amazon

17945240R00122